Electronic Publishing and Libraries. Planning for the Impact and Growth to 2003

Also available in this series:

Project ELVYN: an Experiment in Electronic Journal Delivery. Facts, Figures and Findings
    edited by Fytton Rowland, Cliff McKnight and Jack Meadows
Networking in the Humanities
    edited by Stephanie Kenna and Seamus Ross
The Value and Impact of Information
    edited by Mary Feeney and Maureen Grieves
National Information Policies and Strategies: An Overview and Bibliographic Survey
    Michael W. Hill
Changing Information Technologies: Research Challenges in the Economics of Information
    edited by Mary Feeney and Maureen Grieves
Innovation in Information: Twenty Years of the British Library Research and Development Department
    Jack Meadows
Teaching Information Skills: A Review of the Research and its Impact on Education
    edited by Rick Rogers
Decision Support Systems and Performance Assessment in Academic Libraries
    Roy Adams, Ian Bloor, Mel Collier,
    Marcus Meldrum and Suzanne Ward
Information Technology and the Research Process
    edited by Mary Feeney and Karen Merry
Information UK 2000
    edited by John Martyn, Peter Vickers and Mary Feeney
Scholarly Communication and Serials Prices
    edited by Karen Brookfield
Scholarship and Technology in the Humanities
    edited by May Katzen
Multimedia Information
    edited by Mary Feeney and Shirley Day

Electronic Publishing and Libraries.
Planning for the Impact and Growth to 2003

Compiled by David J Brown
DJB Associates

BOWKER
SAUR

London • Melbourne • Munich • New Jersey

British Library Cataloguing in Publication Data
A catalogue record for this book is available from the British Library.

Library of Congress Cataloging-in-Publication Data
A catalog record for this book is available from the Library of Congress.

Published by Bowker-Saur, a division of Reed Elsevier (UK) Limited
Maypole House, Maypole Road
East Grinstead, West Sussex RH19 1HU, UK
Tel: +44 (0) 1342 330100 Fax: +44 (0) 1342 330191
E-mail: lis@bowker-saur.co.uk
Internet Website: http://www.bowker-saur.co.uk/service/

Bowker-Saur is part of REED REFERENCE PUBLISHING

ISBN 1-85739-166-7

Cover design by John Cole
Desktop published by Mary Feeney, The Data Workshop, Bury St Edmunds
Index compiled by Elizabeth Moys
Printed on acid-free paper
Printed and bound in Great Britain by Antony Rowe Ltd, Chippenham, Wiltshire

Contents

Acknowledgements   vii

Executive summary   viii

Section A: Objectives and methodology   1

Section B: Demand-side economics   7
Review of constraints to the development of
electronic publishing   7
Demographics   8
Employment trends   12
Education   14
Research and development funding   20
Research subject growth   31
Library budgets   36
User studies on information behaviour   43
Technology   55
Conclusions   59

Section C: Supply-side economics   63
The present scholarly publishing system   63
Growth in output of information   68
The information industry overall   71
Printed publications   74
Electronic publications   103
Optical publications   113
Broadcast technologies   132
Telecommunications-based services   134
Other technologies   144

**Section D: Integrated forecasts of established
and new scholarly media**   151

Section E: Legal deposit issues   165

Section F: Requirement for data and economic models   169

Section G: Conclusions and recommendations   171

Bibliography and reading list   175

Appendices   179

Abbreviations   187

Index   189

Acknowledgements

This book emerged out of a project initiated by the British Library's Corporate Research Group. The aim was to provide information which would help in the British Library's assessment of the acquisition policy for digital (as opposed to printed) information within a national legal deposit mandate. Essentially the focus was on how the British Library could fulfil its social responsibility for ensuring the continued availability of scholarly material, in whatever medium and running on whatever hardware, for future generations.

Gratitude is extended to the British Library Research and Development Department whose staff helped greatly with this study, particularly Margaret Croucher. A sizeable vote of thanks is also due to John Martyn who was at one and the same time the project's mentor, adviser, and provider of editorial unity. The charts and tables were brought into consistency through the technical expertise provided by Barrie Christian of Perfect Programmes. The index was compiled by Elizabeth M. Moys. Whilst their various contributions are gratefully acknowledged, any mistakes and errors are those of the author and none of the opinions should be assumed attributable to the British Library.

Executive summary

1. The purpose of this report is to indicate a possible dimension for the scholarly electronic publishing industry by the year 2003. There is nothing magical about the year 2003. It was selected to provide a suitable term within which the dynamics and emerging trends in the information industry can be fully explored. It enables the study to focus on the size and structure of the industry in the early years of the next millennium. The implications on present strategies and planning activities by all parties involved in electronic publishing can be established.

   By taking the eight year term of 1995 to 2003 as the analytical framework it will enable the information community as a whole to plan for the fact that 'change' will become a password and volatility will govern the launch of most information products and services within this period.

2. The emphasis in this study is on scholarly information; research publications which represent a formal record of intellectual achievement in the natural sciences, the social sciences, and the humanities. Real-time services, particularly those in the business and financial sectors—where database publishing has already achieved a substantial industry dimension—are not included in this report. Whilst the emphasis is primarily focused on the UK published output, worldwide trends are also included.

3. Currently the institutional library remains the major purchaser of scholarly publications in printed (book and journal) form. Libraries have suffered from budget constraints in collection development. They have barely been able to keep pace with the output of research literature in conventional form, and the cancellation policies announced by many libraries in recent years demonstrate the extent of their financial problems and that overall collection development programmes are suffering.

4. In essence, research publications suffer from the imbalance between the market forces of 'Supply' and 'Demand'. Supply of published information is created by research scientists striving for international

credibility and respect (and in some cases future financial support) on the basis of the quality of their research effort. A printed article or book is the physical manifestation of this activity. Published information describing the results of research effort has been growing in the 1970s and 1980s at rates which have paralleled international investment in R&D, particularly research conducted within academia.

Demand, on the other hand, is determined at a local or institutional level, and has been based on the ability of the librarian to convince local financial officers that the library warrants additional support. The arguments available bolstering this plea are often without solid foundation, and other conflicting funding projects are frequently supported as they are more able to provide quantified cost/benefit analysis.

5. Superimposed on this imbalance between Supply and Demand is now a new element. The introduction of New Media is straining the budgets of libraries even more. Figure 1 overleaf demonstrates that these new media depend on the same collection development budget as books and journals, and in competing for a growing share of this budget exacerbate the problems facing conventional book and journal publishing.

6. Ultimately each publication, whether traditional or new media, in order to remain commercially viable and therefore to survive, needs its revenue stream to exceed break-even on a prolonged basis unless a justifiable case for cross-subsidization can be made. The break-even in print publishing has remained fairly static in recent years as publishers have come to the end of the road in cost-cutting on the print editions, but still the sales and subscriptions have continued to slide, with journal subscriptions in particular declining at 3-5 per cent per annum. This continued erosion in revenues means that within five years a large number of scientific journals published by the commercial sector will cease publication, for financial rather than editorial reasons. The research communication sector is approaching crisis.

7. The new media, in drawing upon the same 'pot of gold' which supports printed books and journals, add to commercial risks. Though the past few years have seen a crop of forecasts which indicate a healthy growth profile for each medium in turn, what is missing is an integration of these separate forecasts, and an integration which sets

these forecasts against the basic social environmental factors on which publishing is essentially dependent. This report explores such an integrated approach. It suggests that the concept of Supply and Demand must be in balance, and that the total cost of the New Media must not exceed an amount which society can sustain or afford.

Figure 1: *Balance of traditional and new media publications during the 1990s*

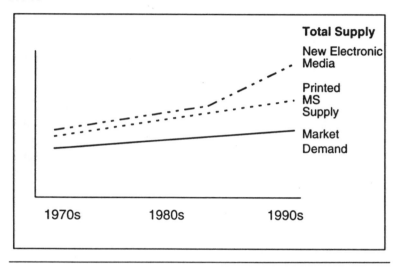

8. Were this competition for the same pot of gold the sole challenge facing print publications some accommodation would be reached (downsizing the likely market size for each medium). However there is a new and more vigorous challenge emerging on the networks. The growth of Internet and World Wide Web has created a sea-change in the information search and retrieval habits of some researchers. In physics and to some extent mathematics, the traditional culture of relying on preprint and reprint distribution to keep colleagues aware of recent achievements has resulted in a new e-print exchange system (electronic preprints). Researchers can search a large file for relevant items and download them to the local terminal/printer for free and instantaneously. The cost and speed advantages over the printed equivalent have given rise to suggestions that within a matter of years

the whole system of information dissemination within the sciences will be based around the Internet and the emerging 'superhighways'. The role of quality control, a key function of the publisher, will be undertaken within and for the research groups by moderators—their duties being similar to those of the traditional editor.

9. It could be argued that the research community can only sustain a given amount of research literature, or that a balance is achieved over time in the average amount of research data which any given subject area can generate, dependent on the number of active researchers. The averages may differ between disciplines, reflecting the differing nature of the subjects and their reliance on published information as a crucial research asset. This would suggest a correlation over time between numbers of researchers and numbers of articles/books produced. Whilst this may have been true in the past, when only books and journals offered the main outlet mechanisms, this is no longer the case when multimedia and network publishing systems are available as alternatives. These new media systems rely on the integration of information published in other forms (text, sound, animation, moving images) to create new 'publications'. The amount of original data may be minimal; the value of the new system lies in the (re)packaging of information into alternative formats to allow a wider group of users access to and benefit from the source material.

10. Therefore, the future of research information will be driven not only by the growth in R&D funding (a function of the national and international research effort), but also by the imagination of new information players who are prepared to repackage information in new ways. This is likely to stress library budgets to such an extent that the commercial fabric of research publishing will probably be substantially altered by the year 2003.

11. One interpretation could be that the 1990s will see the 'valley of death' syndrome. The next few years will see a decline in the printed subscriptions, but before increased revenues from electronic or optical publications can be received, sufficient to support the same publishing infrastructure as now, a period of low profitability and low margins will take place. Leaner and fitter (and fewer traditionalist) information producers will take on the new challenges. Such a structural change in the industry has important repercussions on the balance between print and new media. It also has importance for the

survival of the book and journal publishing industry in its current form and size.

12. A sophisticated approach to the interaction between new and existing media as competitive forces in the marketplace is needed. This is the 'economic modelling' approach which has so far been largely ignored by the information industry. There are some basic premises which such a modelling approach needs to consider; the proposition being that new methods of information access will plateau (in terms of subscribers) much more quickly than in the past, and that linear extrapolation is not realistic. There is a need for a relevant methodology into which the data and projections described in the following report can be inserted. At present no such accepted methodology is available.

SECTION A

Objectives and methodology

The past has revealed to me the structure of the future.
Pierre Teilhard de Chardin, 'Letters from a Traveller'.

Objectives

This report draws together a number of separate attempts at forecasting the impact of the emerging electronic publishing system.

Not only will the present size and estimates of the future size of the various publishing systems, both conventional (printed) and evolving (electronic, optical, network-based), be included in this assessment, but also the speed of migration of products from one form to another will be appraised. The reason for including the present system is that this gives us a standard or scale against which to measure the true impact of electronic publishing (EP) in future years. It enables us to assess whether the impact will be marginal or whether it will affect the fundamentals of STM (Scientific, Technical, Medical) research information dissemination.

The focus is essentially on the UK, though the international nature of scholarly publishing in general means that a global perspective will be adopted when reviewing the supply-side of the information equation.

The statistics collected in this report will help guide the UK information industry through the maze of printed versus electronic information distribution systems, and give an indication of the scale of the problem of creating and handling electronic information in the next decade.

Background

The diffuse nature of the information business, and the lack of quantification of core parts of the industry, makes it difficult to provide projections with any great degree of accuracy. Some of the problems facing crystal ball gazing for this particular industry are summarized below:

Lack of consistency in forecasting

There are many studies which report on specific parts of the information business, but in providing projections for the future fail to take into account the need for an overall assessment of the impact which each, individually, will have on the other (competing) media. Game Theory addresses the challenge of seeing the information industry as an interconnected and interrelated series of products and services. Forecasting just one aspect in isolation leads to the probability that a too enthusiastic assessment may be given, and the sum of such enthusiasms does not equate with the likely overall market (funding) position.

A further complication is that each forecast uses different bases to measure growth. Providing a common measure for comparative growth assessment is not easy.

Balancing supply (output) with demand (purchasing ability)

This is the nub of the study; ideally there should be a comprehensive and integrated assessment of both supply-side and demand-side economics. In principle there is a balance between the academic and research information which society is capable of producing and that which the same society is able to acquire through purchase. This raises the issue of budgetary constraints, which has been addressed in the Follett Report into UK university libraries (*Follett Review*, 1993).

The speed of techno-market change

The problem of balancing supply with demand is made even more complex by the speed of change in scholarly publishing. New media and services are being promoted now which were not even conceived of as recently as 1990, such as DataDiscman, publishing on the Internet, integrated document delivery systems, and extensive multimedia publishing on CD-ROMs (Compact Disc-Read Only Memory). Nor is the rate of change likely to slow down. By the end of the next decade there could be a wide range of new information systems which are not yet even on the drawing board. Forecasting the impact of these with any precision is clearly impossible.

It should perhaps be pointed out that the 'Information UK 2000' view, in contrast, concluded that, 'Most of the innovations which will have penetrated to any great depth by 2000 should be visible now' (Martyn *et al*, 1990). This, however, was specific to the telecommunications industry. It could also be the case that although the technology may already be available, the whole range of new EP applications is still in the process of being created.

The destabilizing influence of new media

Printed publishing has grown faster than the ability of institutional libraries to buy, resulting in an increased rate of title deselection within research libraries. The introduction of new electronic publishing systems threatens to further destabilize the situation. New media are being used to disseminate new editorial content, rather than duplicating content published in another form. This is particularly so with multimedia CD-ROMs and CD-I (Compact Disc-Interactive), and with broadband telecommunications/network publishing.

These new media are adding to the amount of information published on a regular basis but they do not attract a new source of funds with which to purchase them. They compete with conventional books and journals for a share of the restricted materials budgets.

Commercial issues

Established publishing systems—notably scholarly journal publishing—are also likely to suffer major change as publishers wrestle with the continuing decline in subscriptions which is bringing them inexorably closer to the break-even levels below which journal publishing will become commercially unviable. Within the next few years, this situation will need to be addressed by some international 'names', particularly those with many 'twigged' and specialist journal titles. Some of the larger publishing houses have already been driven out of the monograph (book) publishing business for commercial reasons.

There is no study which presents effective financial models of STM journal publishing. The comparative costs of 'electronic journal' versus 'printed journal' publishing are still unclear (Royal Society *et al*, 1993). It is also unclear whether or not the new document delivery systems will survive if their very success drives out of existence the journals on which they depend for their services.

International (supply) versus UK (demand) factors

Academic and research publishing is generated in a global context, and most of the material published is potentially of interest to the UK library community. However, the international supply is led by factors which are totally unrelated to the ability of UK libraries to buy material. The latter is often more a reflection of changing government policy, UK-specific demographic features, and the national economy. This presents a further problem to the UK library community.

Methodology

This study has involved several phases.

Specific forecasts

Reports containing forecasts of the development of various component parts of the information industry have been collected, and relevant statistics extracted, to present a unified approach to the forecast of volumes of printed and electronic publication by the year 2003.

This is essentially an extrapolation based on 'Supply-side Economics'. It is what the existing and new age 'publishers' envisage for the industry over the next ten years. A list of the main reports surveyed is given in the Bibliography at the end of the report.

Background data collection

A second phase has been the collection of statistics of the background against which academic and research publishing will take place over the next ten years. The emphasis here is on demographic, educational and R&D statistics, libraries, and forecasts of these. They provide the 'Demand-side Economics'. They will dictate whether society can support the size of the publishing industry listed under *Specific forecasts* above.

Forecast project

A third approach has been to take all the forecasts which exist and provide a 'best fit' for each electronic new medium. This may in certain instances ignore established forecasts, or modify them in view of constraints set by the factors listed under *Background Data Collection*.

Integration

Ideally the Supply and Demand side assessments would balance out. Where this does not occur, a sizing down (or up) of one or other side of the equation is necessary. The determinant is the market (*Background data*) as this is the ultimate source of the funding.

Procedures

- Meetings were held with Professor Jack Meadows (Loughborough University), David Pullinger (then at the Institute of Physics, currently electronic publishing manager at *Nature*), Dennis Pilling (APC, Boston Spa), John Martyn and Harry East (University of Westminster) and Marc Fresko (consultant) to obtain their views and input.

  Discussions were also held with British Library staff, notably with Margaret Croucher who has been very supportive throughout with background information. A particular vote of gratitude is extended to John Martyn who has guided this project along from its inception.

- Interviews were held with a wide range of STM publishers to see how they come to terms with the new electronic publishing opportunities open to them. This included a visit to some of the key publishers based in New York, who have a distinctive North American view on electronic publishing developments.

- The contents from a list of reports have been analyzed to provide the present view on the growth opportunities for the various electronic publishing media over the next decade. These reports are identified in the Bibliography at the end of this study.

- The impact of new electronic and optical media on the scholarly, particularly the scientific, technical and medical sectors, was assessed, on the basis that these sectors are to the fore in experiments with new media for information dissemination. However, the consumer and entertainment sectors deserve a special analysis of their own, and are not treated here.

References

Follett Review (1993) *Joint Funding Councils' Libraries Review Group: Report.* (Chairman: Sir Brian Follett). Bristol: HEFCE.

Martyn, J., Vickers, P., and Feeney, M. (eds.) (1990) *Information UK 2000.* London: Bowker Saur.

Royal Society, British Library and Association of Learned and Professional Society Publishers (1993) *The scientific, technical and medical information system in the UK.* British Library R&D Report 6123. London: The Royal Society.

SECTION B

Demand-side economics

If politics is the art of the possible,
research is surely the art of the soluble.
Sir Peter Medawar, 'The Art of the Soluble'.

Review of constraints to the development of electronic publishing

This Section looks at the infrastructural issues which will determine whether there is scope for the support of a healthy and rapidly growing printed and electronics information industry.

If sufficient money were available to sustain all the new information services which are ready for market, or are still under development, then the basic concern which this study addresses may be inappropriate. However, the main thesis is that there is too much information chasing too limited an amount of money, given present publication systems, and that the introduction of new media—particularly if they carry genuine new editorial content—is likely to cause a crisis in the scholarly communication business within the next 5-10 years.

A number of factors are relevant in determining the ability of the Demand-side of the information industry to grow in tandem with the output or Supply of published information. These demand factors are often social, economic or political—macro-level determinants which provide the climate within which a social investment is made in the support services that provide the mechanisms for buying research publications, printed or electronic. It is important to review these factors even though their determination of the size of the information industry might seem at best contextual. They determine the scope for a growing information economy.

Some of these factors include the demographic situation within the country, how this supports an educational infrastructure, whether this in turn leads to a healthy research and development (R&D) environment, the implications this has on the institutional research library, and finally, the impact which technology will have on supporting new developments in acquiring and using information services in future.

Demographics

Population trends

Population growth has both a positive and a negative influence on the demand for electronic publications. On the one hand, an expanding population provides a growing potential market for EP products and services. On the other, a population whose expansion is out of step with economic growth can slip into increasing poverty and reduced social investment in such 'luxuries' as higher education and public/private investment in research and development.

The world's population grew to 1.7 billion in 1900. It is expected to reach 6 billion by the year 2000. A 'saturation level' (in social terms) of between 8 and 15 billion is guestimated depending on how rapidly population stabilization measures succeed. This population growth is taking place almost exclusively in the developing world, and is one of the major stress factors which impact on modern society.

The latest edition of the *Unesco Statistical Handbook* gives a forecast of population growth as follows:

Figure 2: World population trends, 1980-2010

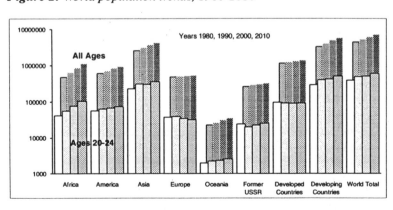

Unesco statisticians anticipate that the world population will grow by 1.5 per cent per annum during the period 1990 to 2010. However, most of this growth is occurring in the 'developing nation' category (+1.8 per cent per annum) which will also account for 80 per cent of the world's population in 2010. The 'developed countries' will increase their population at +0.5 per cent per annum during this same period. The consequence at a global level is that the resources for supporting scientific research and information will be even more restricted to the richer countries. World resources will find other avenues for commitment, with science not necessarily figuring as a key expenditure area.

The 'developed' countries of the world are overwhelmingly the major producers of research information. The following data demonstrate that a few rich countries were responsible for most of the research during the 1970s, and similar studies have shown that the same countries were responsible for most of the output of research publications.

Figure 3*: Total scientists and engineers compared with population figures (1960-70)*

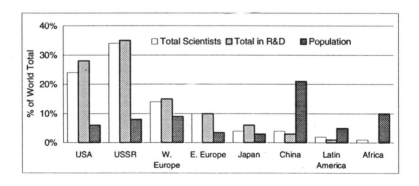

Investigations undertaken by Derek de Solla Price at Yale University in the early 1960s showed that there is a strong and positive correlation between a country's gross national product (GNP) and its support for science. This has been taken a stage further more recently to show that the correlation coefficient between numbers of research papers published and gross domestic product (GDP) is also very high (R=+0.93). There is an elegant simplicity in such a relationship—the more wealthy a country is, the greater the proportion of its resources can be invested in R&D, which in turn creates the need for publications to establish priority for the researchers concerned. Science and publishable information go hand in hand.

Figure 4: Number of research papers published as a function of GDP

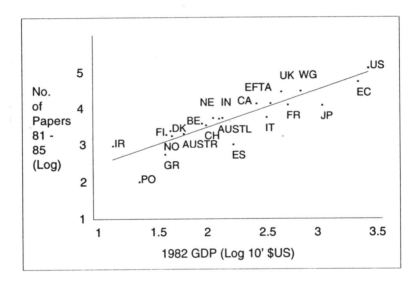

If such relationships are real, it would be necessary for developing countries to increase their economies at a rate much greater than their increase in population levels in order to be in a position to become viable expanding centres for scientific research and discovery. As the following graph illustrates, the proportion of the GNP which is devoted to research in a country increases gradually over time—it is not an explosive growth. In the case of the USA it grew from 0.2 per cent of GNP in 1930 to 3 per cent in 1965.

Figure 5: *National expenditure on R&D in percentage of GNP*

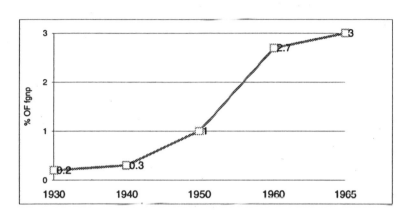

Source: Reviews of National Science Policy: United States, OECD, 1968

World population statistics alone offer no comfort in looking for a more equable balance in scholarly research, which could feed back to a more even distribution in the publication of information, on existing or new media. Certainly not in the short term, as each economy gears itself up gradually to support a higher level of scientific research only after a sustainable population level has been achieved and economic take-off has occurred.

In summary, the above suggests:

- The world population will continue to expand at an annual growth rate of 1.5 per cent.

- Most of this growth will be concentrated in the poorer 'less developed' world (Africa and Asia).

- The developed world has a static population.

- Unless the economic and social conditions of the third world improve, the rich countries will get richer and the poor even more impoverished.

- The number of potential users of electronic information in the year 2003 in the Americas will grow at 0.7 per cent per annum, and within Europe will fall by 1.2 per cent per annum in the important 20-24 age group.

• The USA will have lost 10 per cent of its population in the 20-24 age bracket by 2003, whilst the UK will have lost 25 per cent. West Germany would have lost 30 per cent before East German figures were included in a united Germany.

The overall conclusion is that the population growth alone will not provide the stimulus to new R&D and electronic publishing initiatives. At best the figures for R&D suggest a static level of funding in real terms; more likely is that the demographic trends will work against a dramatic (rather than gradual) growth in global scientific information needs.

Employment trends

European employment trends

As we have seen, the European population in the period up to 2010 is likely to be a declining proportion of the world total. Currently it is 345 million (6.5 per cent). This has fallen from 9.8 per cent in 1960 and will be barely over 4 per cent of the world total in the year 2020.

Some additional aspects of the European population trends are that:

• There has been a marked ageing in population. The over-60s age category will grow from 18 per cent in 1960 to 20 per cent in 1990 and to 28 per cent in 2020 (Source: EUROSTAT).

• Immigration has been responsible for much of the recent increase in the European labour force.

• There has been a growth in the female proportion of the overall labour force. However, Europe has still some way to go to catch up on USA and Japan in this respect; they each have much higher female participation rates in the employment markets.

The following Figure shows how the European index of working-age population compares with that of some other countries for the period up to 2050. Only the USA gives any sign of creating an expanding working population sufficient to fuel a growing R&D platform.

Figure 6: Index of working-age (15-64) population

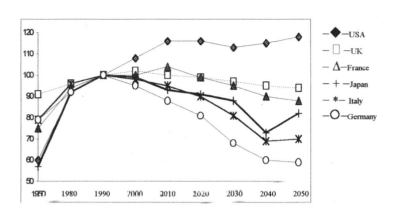

Source: Johnson, P., Our Ageing Population—the implication for business and government, Long Range Planning

Other key points to emerge from an analysis of the demographic situation in Europe were provided by Consulting Trust GmbH in their assessment for the European Commission of the European Information Industry in the year 2000 (1993). Their conclusions were that:

- there will be a growing shortage of young people in most European countries

- there will also be a shortage of IT skills

United Kingdom employment trends

In the UK, several estimates put the population at the beginning of the next century at between 56.9 and 59 million (up to a 7 per cent increase over 1981). As indicated above, there will be a particularly sharp decline in the number of 15-24 year olds. According to *Information UK 2000*, the fall will be 16.8 per cent between 1981 and 2001 (Martyn *et al* 1990).

Again, these figures do not encourage expectations of a sufficient demand for more publications—both conventional and electronic—or expectations of a natural demand-led growth in the STM information market. There is only so much information which any individual can handle. Indications already exist that a large proportion of the scientific community suffers from 'information overload'. It is not likely that the existing numbers of researchers will be able to absorb even more, so that if the appropriate sector of the population is not growing, the uptake of new publications in whatever form must remain limited.

While the overall population itself may not be a factor in creating more demand for STM literature, is it possible that the education sector itself, more particularly the higher education sector, may spearhead such expansion?

Education

International student numbers

Another consideration is the number of students who may currently use research information, or who will move on to become postgraduates and researchers with a greater need for research publications. If the student population is set for rapid growth this may in itself set new demand factors in train to stimulate a growth in research publications.

Table 1 is derived from the latest *Unesco Statistical Yearbook* and gives a comparison of the expenditures of several of the larger countries in support of education.

Though international comparisons are difficult because of local differences in data collection procedures, and Unesco data are not always reliable or up to date, the following table does suggest that the developed countries invest about 5 per cent of their gross national product in education. Approximately 90 per cent of this is current account spending and 10 per cent occurs on capital account.

In the UK approximately £27 billion is directed at the public support of education, a figure which is augmented by the increasing amount of private education.

The *Science and Engineering Indicators* in the USA show the number of first degree conferments made by some of the larger developed countries. In the natural sciences, the USA and India dominate, each

Table 1: Public expenditure on education

Year	Total Educ Expend			Current Educ Expend			Capital Expend
	Amount	% of GNP	% of gov exp	Amount	% of GNP	% of gov exp	
	(in mil)	%	%	(in mil)	%	%	(in mil)
USA (in $)							
1980	182,849	6.7%	-	-	-	-	-
1985	199,373	5.0%	15.5%	182,875	4.6%	16.3%	16,491
1987	227,800	5.1%	11.9%	207,053	4.6%	12.0%	20,710
1988	251,921	5.2%	12.4%	228,864	4.7%	12.6%	23,000
1989	275,044	5.3%	12.4%	247,530	4.8%	12.4%	27,400
GERMANY (In DM)							
1980	70,099	4.7%	9.5%	60,588	4.1%	-	9,541
1985	83,691	4.6%	9.2%	75,566	4.1%	9.4%	8,125
1987	88,445	4.4%	9.0%	79,906	4.0%	9.2%	8,530
1988	89,787	4.3%	8.8%	81,123	3.8%	8.9%	8,624
1989	92,631	4.1%	8.8%	83,481	3.7%	8.9%	9,150
1990	98,412	4.1%	8.6%	88,499	3.6%	8.7%	9,913
FRANCE (in FF)							
1980	142,099	5.0%	-	131,441	4.7%	-	10,650
1985	269,191	5.8%	-	254,433	5.4%	-	14,758
1988	310,485	5.4%	-	288,647	5.1%	-	21,838
1989	329,051	5.4%	-	305,802	5.0%	-	23,245
1990	351,867	5.4%	-	327,427	5.1%	-	24,440
1991	388,819	5.8%	-	356,336	5.3%	-	32,483
UNITED KINGDOM (in £)							
1980	12,856	5.6%	13.9%	12,094	-	-	-
1985	17,501	4.9%	-	16,764	-	-	-
1987	20,401	4.9%	-	19,596	-	-	-
1988	22,148	4.8%	-	21,375	-	-	-
1989	24,102	4.7%	-	22,829	-	-	-
1990	26,677	4.9%	-	-	-	-	-

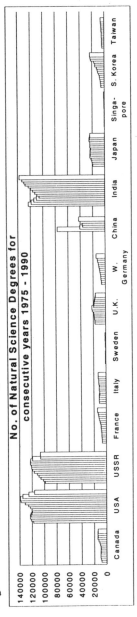

Figure 7: Natural Science Bachelors Degrees, by country, 1975-90

Figure 8: Engineering Bachelors Degrees, by country, 1975-90

Source: Science Resources Studies Division, National Science Foundation, unpublished tabulations.

having over 125,000 graduates annually. The UK compares with France, Italy and Germany, all having in the region of 12-16,000 natural science students per annum.

By comparison, the engineering graduates figures show the UK falling behind France and Italy; USSR (with nearly 300,000 graduates at that stage) led the international engineering graduate league table. Japan also exceeded the USA with 77,000 as against 70,000. These comparative statistics are shown in Figures 7 and 8. (Note that the National Science Foundation (NSF) data do not provide equivalent figures for medical students.)

European student enrolments

Using the same reference source, the enrolment of students per 100,000 population in Europe shows a varied pattern. Nordic countries and the larger EU countries are high in the student enrolment league table, though the UK has a moderate position (about 2,000 students per 100,000 head of population).

Figure 9: European student levels per 100,000 population

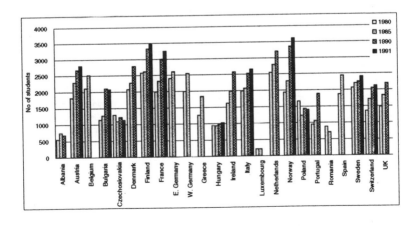

UK student levels

UK student numbers have increased from 517,000 to 811,000 (or 57 per cent) within the period 1988/89 to 1992/93. Estimates for 1993/94 are 900,000 (*Follett Review*, 1993). Government projections call for a further rise to 1,170,000 by the year 2000.

Projections made by the Institute of Manpower Studies show that the number of graduates will increase by 5 per cent over the 1990-1993 period, and may then level off because there will be fewer 18 year olds.

The UK government's aim of doubling the number of higher education students over the next 25 years cannot be achieved without a much greater participation rate, with more 18 year olds going on to college/university and more mature students attending higher education courses.

The rapid growth in student enrolment has been the greatest since Robbins, though it coincides with difficulties in the HEI (Higher Education Institution) infrastructure and particularly in library provision (*Follett Review*, 1993). In order to cope with some of the new pressures, particularly from mature students, there will of necessity be an increase in education at home, self tuition, and remote learning, and the emergence of 'electronic universities' (Martyn *et al*, 1990).

Figure 10: *Number of home and EC undergraduate students (FTE)*

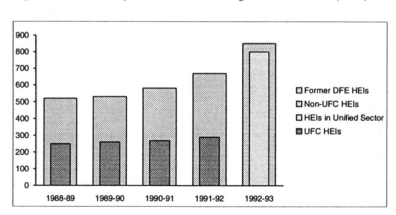

Source: USR Volume 1, PCFG Monitoring Base

Extrapolating the trends to the year 2000 (using data provided by the Central Statistical Unit) gives the following chart.

Figure 11: Changes in student numbers and demography, 1987-2000 (GB only)

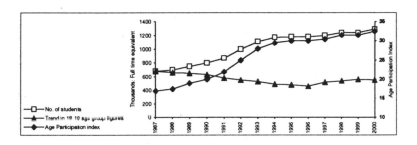

On the basis of trends during the 1980s it seems likely that the number of full-time students will increase by about 20 per cent between 1981/82 and 1999/2000. The number of part-time students will grow by 80 per cent during the same period.

Both student sectors will have an impact on the sort of published material which will be generated during this period. Demand for more interactive, self-testing modules using latest new media technology, is a probable outcome. This will reduce the pressure to appoint a much greater number of qualified teachers to support the larger student population.

This is one of the key factors which an analysis of education trends highlights—as more student enrolments are planned in the UK, for example, the impact which resource allocation in favour of education will have in comparison with research will need to be considered. More resources ploughed into providing more young people with a degree which will enable them to enter the employment market might be at the expense of supporting advanced research in academia.

Research and development funding

The distribution of scientific and technical R&D is uneven between regions and countries. Over four-fifths of R&D activities are concentrated in a handful of industrialized countries. In 1990 expenditure on R&D as a percentage of gross national product was 2.9 per cent for the industrialized world (slightly less in the UK), whilst many developing countries could barely manage one-tenth of this level (Unesco, 1993).

The following figure shows the estimated number of scientific and technical staff per million population in the various regions.

Figure 12: Worldwide scientific and technical manpower estimates

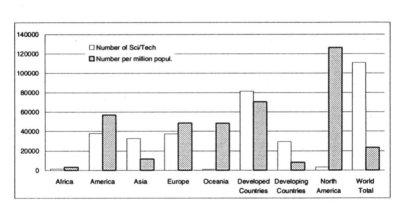

Source: Unesco Statistical Yearbook, 1992.

Four out of five of the world's scientific and technical personnel are based in developed countries. North America alone has nearly half of these.

R&D worldwide

During the past two centuries, science has flourished in comparatively few regions—chiefly Europe, North America and Japan. For many reasons the Third World fell behind, and (with some brilliant exceptions) still suffers from a lack of knowledge-based development.

While the developed countries share the same conflicts in resource allocation, they also share a fundamental tradition of support for science and technology within the industrialized society. In the developing world no such tradition exists. There is a lack of extensive formal education which provides the bedrock on which R&D can be based. But, more fundamentally, there is a need to develop value systems which assign a high degree of prestige to the pursuit of scholarship. In their absence, the developing world is unlikely to stimulate a future massive expansion in R&D, and fuel the need for more research publications.

The last century has seen an acceleration of the growth of knowledge. The last few decades have been variously hailed as the Atomic Age, the Space Age, the Age of Electronics and Informatics, the Age of New Biology, the Age of New Materials and the Age of Understanding the Universe; these titles reflecting both the growth and the diversity of scientific activity and information. As a consequence of this burgeoning development, science now exhibits a number of new features:

- *Interdisciplinarity*: Major scientific progress is no longer solely in the core disciplines of mathematics, physics or chemistry, but more often develops through a multidisciplinary approach leading to growth areas such as molecular biology, genetic engineering, biotechnology, etc.

- *Basic versus Applied*: There is a closer interaction between basic and applied research, particularly in engineering and agriculture. Science now enjoys a much greater symbiotic relationship with technology.

- *Speed*: Scientific discoveries are put to practical use more rapidly, often before the publication of the original research results.

- *Defence*: Defence spending has been a major stimulus to national R&D efforts. The fear of terrorism in some countries has more recently been an incentive to search for scientific and technological protection.

- *Megascience*: The past fifty years have seen the emergence of concentrated or globally distributed but interlinked research establishments which are staffed by large teams of scientists, and whose large costs are not borne by any one country (such as high energy physics, satellite and launch systems, the human genome).

Science is no longer a standalone activity at the fringes of society, but one which is closely entwined with medical, industrial, agricultural and other production sectors, in such a manner and to such an extent that science pervades society as a whole. This has led to a change in the way that R&D is funded. Throughout the history of modern science a significant proportion of research has been carried out in higher educational institutions. Now we have the emergence of industrial research laboratories, such as Bell Labs, or Xerox at Menlo Park. Today a large and growing part of the expenditure on R&D is provided by industry; and by government in such areas as defence spending, the provision of infrastructural and surveying facilities, and large programmes such as space, meteorological and oceanographic research. University research may seem to be relegated to the background, and may indeed be so in terms of overall financial allocations, although it still continues to be the principal venue for basic science.

The megascience era may lead to an attenuation of resources for 'small science'. Achieving a balance between small and big science is one of the main challenges facing the R&D funding agencies over the next few years.

Another challenge is that created by the allocation of resources stemming from the 'peace dividend'. With the end of the cold war, and the global move towards a market economy, some of the reduction in defence allocations may be available for civilian purposes. However, economic conditions which have emerged over the past few years in both the world's wealthiest and poorest economies have meant that there has been no increase in assistance by the rich to the poor countries (ultimately—and in the long term—boosting their R&D efforts) nor increased funding for science in the developed world. A second constraint is that governments are finding it more and more difficult in an age of increasing decentralization and consumerism to levy taxes to finance central government activities such as basic R&D . The corollary is that investment is likely to be oriented more towards applied research and technological innovation, which are nearer to the consumer market place.

Some of the regional differences in R&D are described below.

R&D in North America

Annual R&D spending in the USA, Canada and Mexico combined totalled about $165 billion in the 1990-1992 period. This served a combined population of 400 million, with a GDP of $6 trillion. The following table shows a comparison of the R&D funding among the three North American countries. (The data may imply that the more industrialized a country, the more R&D-intensive is the economy and the more private-firm-oriented is the R&D activity.)

Table 2: *Selected comparative indicators, 1990-1992*

	USA (1992)	Canada (1991)	Mexico (1991)
Total R&D Spending (US $ bil)	157	8	1
Total R&D as a % of GDP	2.7%	1.4%	0.1%
% of total R&D (a) financed by industry	51%	42%	7%
(b) performed by industry	70%	55%	na
% of total R&D performed by universities	18%	25%	31%
Population (1990 in mil)	250	27	86
GNP per capita (1990) US $'000s	21.8	20.5	2.5

Source: World Science Report, 1993, Unesco

Within the USA specifically, research and development has developed in distinct phases.

- From 1960-1968 there was the period of robust growth—the 'Space Race' era.

- From 1968-1975 there was a substantial real decrease due to inflationary pressures

- From 1975-1985 there were spurts of activity which coincided with the military technology build-up under President Reagan and a growth in life science support.

- Since 1985 the US government funding on R&D has kept up with inflation but not much more.

Though there has been a simultaneous growing awareness by the private sector of the need for more R&D effort, there have also been some real problems. Firstly, the increasing cost of undertaking R&D efforts is becoming evident, resulting in a greater interest in multinational cooperative 'megascience' projects. Secondly, there is the danger that funding short-term and expedient projects will take priority over basic research.

'National economic competitiveness' has become an important North American stimulant for R&D funding. Funding will probably grow over the 1990s whenever and wherever economic conditions permit. This is against a background of substantially greater approval of science and technology in the USA than in most other countries. European nations lag behind the US, and Japan's approval of science is the lowest in the industrial world. There is also an age dimension. In most countries there is an inverse relationship between age and scientific knowledge, with younger adults knowing more science on average than their elders.

During the period 1985-1992, the USA had a slower growth rate in R&D funding in constant dollars (about 1 per cent pa) than in the period 1975-1985 (about 5-6 per cent pa). Industrial R&D has grown more slowly in recent years whilst academic spending has risen more quickly. The proportion of the GDP spent on all R&D dropped slightly from 2.8 per cent in 1985 to 2.6 per cent in 1992 (see Figure 13).

Within the USA support for science funding has therefore stalled. Links between public sector research and national economic goals are being emphasized. The strong US investment in biological and medical research continues but with abated growth. Defence research and development is decreasing. Commercially relevant research, sponsored by government, is increasing while corporate support has declined during the recent recession. Vigorous debate proceeds about the comparative priorities and rising costs of 'Big Science' and technology such as the space station and the superconducting super collider. Two decades ago the support for physical and engineering sciences was much greater than that for the life sciences. Now the fields are funded at about the same level.

Figure 13: *US R&D effort, 1992*

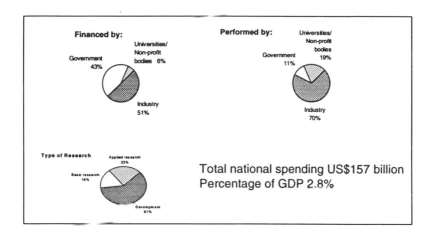

Total national spending US$157 billion
Percentage of GDP 2.8%

Source: National Science Foundation, Oct. 1992

Figure 14: *US government funding for basic and applied research by broad field*

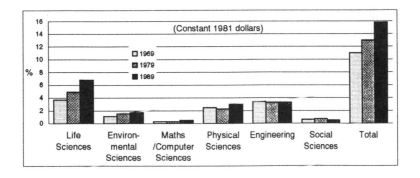

Historically, military research accounted for more than half of the total government investment in R&D. Although this component is declining and is expected to decline further in future, military applications will continue to attract significant funding for R&D in the USA. Nevertheless, the impact of the changes within the defence R&D budget will be felt in a large number of universities and research stations. The impacts will also reverberate among the high technology firms which have traditionally lived off the defence, energy and space programmes.

A major reappraisal is underway in the USA regarding the scope, level, priorities and geographical distribution of support for science at academic institutions. There was about $19 billion invested in 1992, a tripling in scale over 30 years. There are now about 150-200 major research universities in the USA, two-thirds being state-funded and one-third private, together accounting for about 90 per cent of all academic R&D. Greater selectivity is being urged by the President's Advisers on Science and Technology, and programmes which relate more clearly to advancing economic competitiveness are attracting greater federal support. Some of the minor universities have become financially stretched. Links between universities on the one hand and industry and State governments on the other are growing, partly to secure more funds, partly to emphasize technology transfer for the economic good.

The integrity of researchers has also come under scrutiny in the US recently, with claims of plagiarism, fabrication and falsification of results being made in the press. Although this is not yet a major problem, some attempts are being made to confront the issue, such as a more frequent requirement in public-funded research for the individuals to disclose potential conflicts. The stimulus for dishonesty must lie in the fact that with the large pool of available researchers and the scarcity of research funds, only about one in four or five grant applications is receiving support.

R&D in Europe

Within Europe there are a number of overall R&D trends:

- R&D is seen as important to maintain economic advantage (as with the US)

- Emphasis is being placed on R&D effort by small and medium sized enterprises (SMEs)

- Efforts are being made to maximize cost/benefit from R&D programmes

- International cooperation is increasingly important in funding 'Megascience'

- Education and training of scientists has a high priority

There is some variation among these themes between individual countries. France has a long-term target of increasing its expenditure on R&D from 2.4 per cent in 1991 to 3 per cent as soon as possible. Within Germany there has been a major reappraisal whereby the centralized approach adopted in the eastern part has been brought into line with the decentralized west German R&D funding. Small and medium sized companies are given special direct and indirect government aid. Germany invests 2.6 per cent of its GDP on R&D, with civil activities responsible for 89 per cent of the total, and defence R&D some 11 per cent.

Within Italy the aim is to raise R&D to a level comparable with its larger European neighbours, and investment in the research infrastructure is seen as an immediate priority. In 1991 total R&D was 1.4 per cent of the GDP, with 92 per cent spent on civil and 8 per cent on defence.

Table 3 compares and contrasts the R&D activity within the key European countries and with the USA and Japan.

Supporting these national commitments is the European Union itself. The R&D programme has been largely grouped together under the Framework Programme. This has the aim of strengthening the scientific and technological basis of European industry and encouraging it to become more competitive at the international level. It started in the early 1980s, and the Fourth Framework programme for the years 1995 to 1998 is now underway.

The Third Framework programme had a budget of some £5 billion, and operated in three areas—enabling technologies (informatics), management of natural resources, and management of intellectual resources. The budget represents 5 per cent of the overall budget of the European Communities. The Fourth Framework programme has a budget of approximately £10 billion. Among its objectives are reduction of the fragmentation of R&D efforts, and improvement of the application of science in the interests of economic and commercial success.

In addition, the EUREKA programme was set up in 1985, with the objective of being involved in near-market research. Much of the funding

Table 3: Research & Development expenditure by countries

Country	Total GERD (ECU millions)	GERD as % of GDP 1991	GERD per capita population (ECU) 1991	% of GERD 1990 financed by			% GERD 1990 performed by		
				Government	Industry	Other	Government sector	Business enterprise sector	Higher education and other sectors
Belgium	2,722	1.71	272	27.6	70.4	2.0	6.1	72.6	21.3
Denmark	1,675	1.59	325	45.5	46.8	7.7	19.1	55.0	25.9
Germany	35,519	2.58	445	37.2	59.9	2.9	15.2	68.4	16.4
Greece	402	0.70	39	68.9	19.4	11.7	42.4	22.3	35.3
Spain	3,730	0.87	96	45.1	47.4	7.4	21.3	57.8	20.9
France	23,511	2.42	412	48.3	43.5	8.2	24.2	60.4	15.4
Ireland	340	0.97	96	29.0	60.0	11.0	16.2	60.7	23.0
Italy	12,821	1.38	224	51.5	43.7	4.8	20.9	58.3	20.7
Netherlands	4,630	2.00	307	45.1	51.1	3.8	18.1	56.2	25.7
Portugal	399	0.72	41	61.8	27.0	11.1	25.4	26.1	48.4
UK	18,435	2.26	320	35.8	49.5	14.8	14.0	66.6	19.3
Eur 12	104,184	2.02	302	41.2	51.7	7.1	17.4	64.5	18.1
USA	124,559	2.78	493	47.1	50.6	2.3	11.0	69.9	19.1
Japan	77,700	2.86	627	16.1	77.9	6.0	8.0	75.5	16.6

comes from the national governments. This programme is therefore much less centralized than other EU action programmes, and adopts more of a 'bottom up' approach. There are nearly 700 EUREKA projects in operation covering nine different high-tech areas. Finally, there are some intergovernmental research organizations which emphasize specific topics. For example, CERN (Centre Européenne de Recherche Nucléaire) has achieved high success in its area of nuclear research, as has the European Molecular Biology Laboratory in its expanding area. The European Space Agency has its programme of cooperative space research and provides satellite launchers.

In summary, the intergovernmental research organizations are mainly concerned with basic research, the EC programmes embrace pre-competitive research, whilst EUREKA activities belong to the near-market research category.

R&D in the United Kingdom

A radical recent departure from the government's policy, in which near-market R&D was considered to be the responsibility of industry, is seen by the government's intention to support some promising research lines which would otherwise fail to get commercial backing. The Foresight Programme announced in March 1994, with its 15 panels of experts evaluating and reporting back on what they feel to be the biggest developments likely to occur in their respective fields over the next 20-30 years, is one example of this.

Research grants are awarded to peer-reviewed projects by seven sector-based Research Councils, and separate Higher Education Research Councils support the universities in England, Wales, Scotland and Northern Ireland.

In 1991 the total R&D spend, of which 56 per cent was civil and 44 per cent defence related, represented 2.3 per cent of the GDP.

R&D in Japan

Two factors have become critical to Japan's success as an industrial society. The first is the direct involvement of the government in promoting R&D, and the other is the exceptional performance of the private sector in adopting and applying R&D results in a commercial context.

The government operates a vast network of agencies that formulate and implement R&D in a variety of productive sectors. In April 1992 the

Japanese government adopted a resolution entitled *General Guideline for Science and Technology (S&T) Policy.* The main areas supported included Basic and Leading S&T; S&T for human coexistence and S&T for enriching life and society. Japan's investment in natural sciences R&D in 1991 was 2.76 per cent of GNP, the highest proportion in the world. In 1990 the government contributed 16.5 per cent of this total. This proportion has been falling over the years. The government funding is important nonetheless because it supports the basic research efforts.

It is in the private sector that the real achievement in R&D has occurred. Private sector R&D has trebled over the past decade. This has skewed Japan's infrastructure in that the research facilities are much better in the private sector than at either universities or government funded research centres. Almost three-quarters of private sector R&D is aimed at developmental projects (71.8 per cent) with only 6.4 per cent on basic research. In the past 10 years the share of the R&D personnel in private companies increased by 7 per cent, whilst in research institutions and universities it decreased by 2 per cent and 5 per cent respectively.

The result is that the overall environment for basic research is believed to be inferior in Japan to that which exists in the USA or Europe, except in specific areas such as electronics and communications. This has contributed to the rejection by young people of S&T as a career, and the demand for scientists is as a result potentially outstripping the supply. It has also led to a growth in R&D in various industries in Japan, as shown in Figure 15.

The output of research publications is affected by the need to maintain competitive advantage within companies, so that there is a less liberal open publication system.

Summary

What we are seeing is a universal trend towards R&D becoming more market-focused. The ivory tower image much cherished in the UK in former decades is now being swept aside by all the developed countries and those research areas where an immediate and demonstrable social or economic return may be generated are getting the lion's share of the public R&D funds. This is changing the nature of the global R&D effort, with a diminishing share going to those basic research areas upon which much of the new applications are based.

Figure 15: Private sector R&D expenditure by industry in Japan

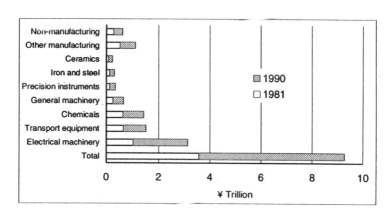

Research subject growth

One possible measure of research output is the number of published articles in the mainstream international scholarly journals. A view of trends is provided by the data collected by NFAIS (National Federation of Abstracting and Indexing Services) in the USA (see Table 4). NFAIS has an international membership of secondary bibliographic database providers.

An alternative source is the data collected by the Institute for Scientific Information Inc. (ISI). This company is at the forefront of bibliometrics within science, and its database enables a range of information to be compiled on growth in article production. However, it is a not fully representative source in the sense that it only covers approximately 7-8,000 journals (out of a universe of 126,000) and half of these are social science and humanities titles. New journals are excluded until such time as they become established, which tends to reduce coverage of many 'twigged' information areas. ('Twigged' titles are those journals which are published on behalf of a new and emerging sub-discipline, one which formerly was incorporated within a large and established science area, but felt that its uniqueness demanded its own separate publication forum.)

Table 4: Output of research articles by subject area

	1957	1962	1967	1972	1977	1982	1987	1990	1991	1992	1993*
Am. Assoc. of Retired Persons	0	0	0	0	0	0	2716	3095	2445	3313	3000
Am. Bankers Assoc.	0	0	0	0	0	4000	14377	13836	13600	11750	14000
Am. Economic Assoc.	0	0	0	9300	11200	9400	21700	19913	21196	21949	25000
Am. Inst. of Aeronautics & Astronautics	0	12048	33116	35794	41633	38267	44377	43109	47068	46278	46000
Am. Inst. of Physics	0	0	0	29507	21435	26531	34148	38698	40100	43189	46400
Am. Meteorological Inst.	5000	12000	9000	7200	7200	7200	7200	7200	9000	9000	9000
Am. Petroleum Inst.	11615	21977	29151	32983	70462	90654	67772	83312	81889	84662	84350
Am. Psychological Inst.	9074	8776	14840	24316	26980	36890	43605	51171	51740	57008	58200
Bibliography of the History of Art	0	0	0	0	7669	9200	10000	0	22000	24000	24000
BIOSIS	40060	100858	193108	240006	250148	315024	506020	593225	605706	605249	605000
R.R. Bowker	-	-	-	5000	11800	16613	18225	19498	21292	26600	19200
Chemical Abstracts Service	102525	175138	269293	379048	478225	557447	578597	607630	686717	668268	675000
Defense Tech. Inf. Center	21000	23897	65777	49603	45740	47359	43616	51367	46027	41924	42000
Dept. of Energy	14042	34149	47055	60848	160000	180000	185000	183583	164632	183866	172000
Earthquake Eng. Res. Center	0	0	0	600	1100	2110	2400	2697	2873	3381	2600
Elsevier Science Publishers B.V.	0	0	0	0	217957	255116	235645	397486	354521	372132	372132
Engineering Inf. Inc.	26797	38120	51670	83653	95000	179300	220000	150281	285127	309000	330000
Fachinformationszentrum Karlsruhe	0	0	0	0	0	196000	239000	350000	315000	370190	370000
Faxon Research ServicesInc.	0	0	0	0	0	0	0	0	0	2403495	959280
The Getty Conservation Inst.	0	737	2520	933	1344	2000	1500	2483	3092	3042	3000
Information Access Co.	0	0	0	0	64195	403463	575221	965179	1120679	971153	2000000

INFO-SOUTH	0	0	0	0	0	0	0	14612	12746	11354	13000
INIST/CNRS	148883	251274	367300	470184	545099	372055	495548	454000	675000	732829	675000
INSPEC	16452	39272	71032	132394	135184	187054	46313	258348	259812	257650	270000
Inst. for Sc. Inf.	115367	182771	360056	432842	715146	952344	1079561	1060214	1083028	1143949	1178267
Inst. of Elec. & Electronic Engineers	0	0	0	5473	14305	19000	24200	27854	28864	36396	32000
Inst of Paper Sc. & Tech.	7331	11578	9753	12450	11690	12480	14290	12530	14300	18750	21600
International Translations Centre	0	38217	15571	20000	26079	15649	28173	22888	24431	27426	28000
Migration Inf. & Abstracts Service	0	0	0	0	0	0	1059	1331	1441	1552	1000
Modem Language Assoc.	0	0	25534	46534	44371	39817	43393	45000	42350	50000	50000
National Aeronautics & Space Admin.		11386	107260	81810	96293	76000	79496	91321	82500	78300	81600
National Agric. Lib.	98409	94968	102198	124592	144389	150405	108842	7519	82586	115622	97000
Nat. Center for Post-Traumatic Stress Disorder		0	0	0	0	0	0	1500	2000	1000	1500
Nat. Lib of Medicine	104517	150000	165000	221000	259980	282180	317435	91172	363344	401000	380000
Online Comp. Lib. Cen.	0	0	0	2000000	2000000	2000000	2000000	2000000	2000000	2000000	2000000
Public Affairs Inf. Service	0	0	0	0	0	23600	21000	18500	19700	18400	18000
Philosophy Doc Cen.	0	0	2000	3100	26000	8200	7968	6996	7842	5571	8500
Pop. Inf. Prog.	0	0	0	0	0	24099	7135	9209	7000	8811	9000
Sc. & Tech. Inf. Cen.	0	0	0	0	49994	80998	158780	115000	12355	137547	139000
Sociological Abs.	1015	2957	9460	14064	13800	17918	27620	32864	36000	36642	38950
UMI	25000	27000	28000	28000	54000	83000	630000	1021000	1000000	1200000	1300000
University of Tulsa	0	10816	15519	13112	14431	20705	19826	20062	21685	24332	24000
The H.W. Wilson Co.	0	0	0	0	0	0	560914	588638	590000	755675	956950

Figure 16: *US and world scientific & technical articles, by field, 1973-87*

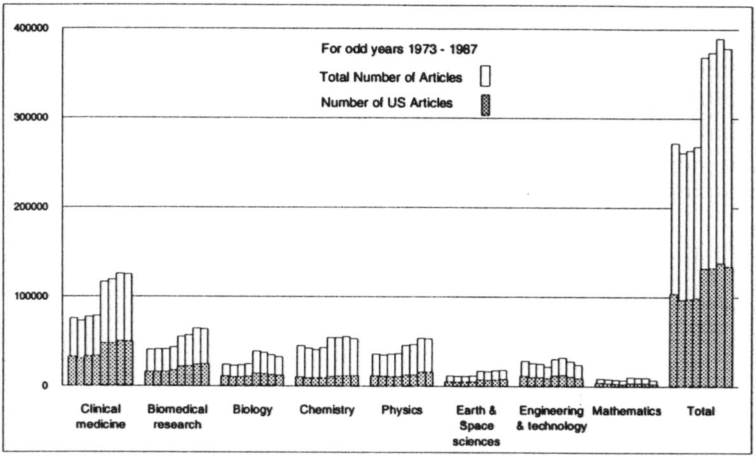

Source: CHI Research Inc., Science & Engineering Indicators Literature Database, 1989

The contribution provided by several countries to the growth in article output is shown in the following two Figures.

There are some dominant areas which represent the core of the public and private funding of scientific research. Biomedical and clinical research generate a great deal of research support and have as a consequence a dominance in the world's output of research information. However, there are few major swings between the subject area support, though gradual trends emerge over time as specific areas gain international visibility. In general there is a cautious and conservative element to the support for subject areas within science—inevitable, some may say, given the large infrastructural investments which have been made over the decades in supporting schools of study in these separate areas.

Figure 17: *Contribution of selected countries to world literature, by field, 1981 & 1987*

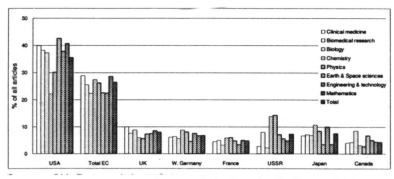

Source: *CHI Research Inc., Science & Engineering Indicators Literature Database, 1989*

Figure 18: *Scientific specialization by region, 1991*

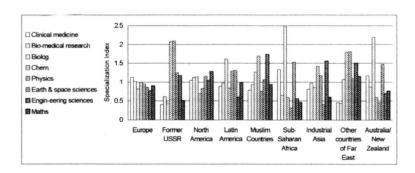

The indicator presented here is the specialization index for eight scientific disciplines; it is the ratio of the country`s world percentage share of publications in one discipline against the world percentage share of the country all disciplines combined (an index figure higher than unity indicates a relative strength specialization of the country, and its relative weakness, lack of specialization, if the figure is less than unity).

Library budgets

> *A library is thought in cold storage.*
> *Lord Samuel, 'A Book of Quotations'.*

Historical perspective

Another vital element is the role of the library. For scholarly titles this remains the main source of funds. Almost 90 per cent of the revenues received by a typical specialist research journal will come from the subscriptions taken out by institutional libraries. The library has been the 'Milch Kuh' on which many parts of the STM journal publishing sector grew fat.

The Golden Age was in the late 1960s and early 1970s. During this period science flourished, particularly in the USA. The 'space race' obliged the federal government to commit large amounts of funding to research, some of which filtered through to the research library. Not only did new journal titles proliferate during this period, but subscriptions to existing titles also increased. Journal publishers could do no wrong. Within 3-4 years of a title's launch publishers were able to reach financial break-even, and the reluctance of librarians to cancel subscriptions to a title meant that each journal became, over time, a small goldmine.

The last two decades have seen an almost universal worldwide falling away from this happy state. The research effort has been modified (see earlier) to become oriented toward the practical needs of society. Research libraries have had their budgets cut, not only because basic scientific research has lost its high status in the political milieu, but also because the library itself has come under scrutiny. No longer is the library seen as the 'citadel of learning', or if it is still viewed as such the concept of the citadel itself has become tarnished. In the UK the percentage of the campus budget controlled by the research library has fallen from over 4 per cent to under 3 per cent during the past decade.

There is much anecdotal information about how badly the libraries are faring. Many US libraries are slashing books and journals budgets by hundreds of thousands of dollars, and relying on resource sharing with other libraries such as through interlibrary loan and document supply to fill the void. Some UK university libraries are also beginning to feel the squeeze. It is part of the move away from a holdings strategy to an access strategy, from buying information 'just in case' it is ever needed to 'just in time' only when the need is felt.

It is against this background that expenditure by libraries on the traditional books/journals and on the new media is entering a new phase, a phase which is difficult to define. It is unclear whether the problems facing the research library budget will hasten or slow down the move towards information packaging within new electronic media. A robust and healthy library budget may provide a reliable source of support for new media developments, particularly those which command a high price because of the extra functionality which is built into them. Without such budgets the new media may not emerge. On the other hand, a tight budget may force libraries to demand a greater efficiency in the new media which is lacking in the (under-utilized) printed book and journal system. Either way there may be just enough support from libraries to cushion the development of more and more new media products during the rest of this decade, at the expense of support given to books and journals.

Types of libraries

There is little commonality between the main types of libraries which purchase STM information. At one extreme is the public library, steeped in tradition and committed to the printed book for circulation and borrowing. At the other are advanced information units within large corporate and commercial businesses, where the accent may be on online searching and where the concept of the 'digital library' is at its closest to realization.

UK public libraries
The total book stock held by public libraries in the UK has remained broadly constant during the 1980s at about 120 million volumes (see Figure 19).

Despite the assertion that public libraries are tradition-bound, and supportive of the book, an analysis by Harry East, published as a CCIS (Centre for Communication and Information Studies) Policy Paper, shows how library authorities have increased their commitment to electronic publications over the period 1985 to 1991 (East, 1991).

UK university libraries
University libraries have provided the solid core of support on which most journal publishers in Europe have survived and profited over the

Figure 19: Expenditure on books by public libraries

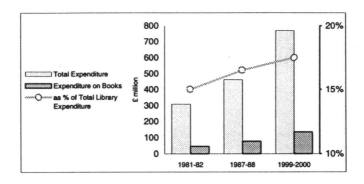

last three decades. However, the library budgets overall have begun to suffer, and consequentially the amount available to spend on collection development has fallen as the prices of published material has risen (see Table 5). It is the severity of this suffering which led to a Libraries Review being commissioned by the Higher Education Funding Councils in the UK, a review which was chaired by Sir Brian Follett. The report of this group's findings was published in December 1993 (*Follett Review*, 1993).

There is no such thing as a typical university library in the UK. There are several main groups, the greatest distinction being between the 'old' universities and the 'new' universities. The latter are the former polytechnics which became universities during the past few years. Because they were polytechnics until recently, their libraries have a profile which reflects the more applied and teaching orientation of these institutions, whereas the 'old' universities often had large and well stocked libraries serving the research community.

Figure 20 illustrates some of the increases in library activity and provision during the past five years. The increase in student numbers and the probably related growth in total loans of materials is striking. The small increases in periodicals acquisition and physical space for readers/users is an indicator of difficulties to come.

Table 5:

Expenditure on 'old' university libraries

	1981-82	1987-88	1999-2000
Expend on Libraries	£64.5 mil	£96.6 mil	£155 mil
Index	100	150	245
% of Total University Exp	3.82%	3.55%	2.82%
Book Expenditure	£10.3 mil	£14.4 mil	£20.0 mil
Index	100	138	193
Price Index Academic Books	100	159	304
Expend on Periodicals	£10.6 mil	£19.2 mil	£34.3 mil
Index	100	182	325
Periodical Price Index	100	199	407

Expenditure on 'new' university libraries

	1985-86	1987-88	1999-2000
Expend on Libraries	£26.4 mil	£29.5 mil	£49.2 mil
Index	100	112	112
% of Total University Exp	4.42%	4.23%	4.25%
Book Expenditure	£4.2 mil	£4.8 mil	£7.1 mil
Index	100	116	171
Price Index Academic Books	100	142	258
Expend on periodicals	£3.6 mil	£4.4 mil	£6.8 mil
Index	100	121	187
Periodical Price Index	100	150	313

A study undertaken by Harry East has again shown the trend in electronic media adoption within universities in the UK based on a sample of a representative number of higher education establishments (East and Tilson, 1993). The growth in support for CD-ROMs during the period 1988 to 1992 has been dramatic, as has been the declining popularity of uncontrolled (in charging terms) remote database searching (which is difficult to budget for accurately in advance). The diagram in Figure 21 would endorse the view that the CD-ROM publishing business has reached 'take-off'.

Figure 20: *Sector profile: percentage changes relating to library provision, 1986-87 to 1991-92*

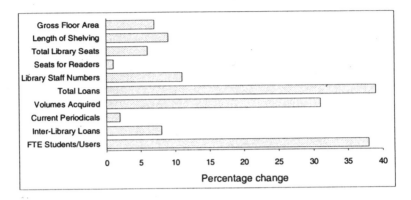

Source: LISU Survey for Joint Libraries Review

Figure 21: *Expenditure by access medium, 1988-92*

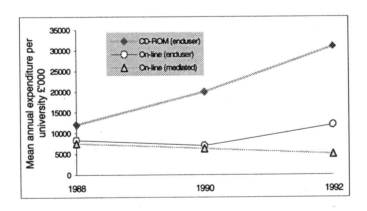

An interesting kink occurs in 1990 when a new service was launched. This is the BIDS -ISI service which was the first of a number of national dataset policies launched by the Higher Education Funding Council (HEFC). The key to this initiative's success was that end users would not be charged for searching the databases; they would be free at the point of usage. The simplicity of the search system and the lack of commercial controls on the payment for the database use (the universities and the HEFC share the costs on an annual license basis) show that electronic publishing can and will be used if the pricing system is hidden. It emphasized the importance of getting the right pricing formula for new media; pricing by connect hour is not conducive to achieving market breakthrough.

Overview

It is clear that both 'old' and 'new' institutions failed to keep pace with the growth in information output. Spending by university libraries on books in the UK amounted to £28 million, and for journals £35 million (1992/3)—according to data supplied to the Follett Review (1993).

The university libraries also failed to generate a constant share of academic budgets. In the UK the proportion of total campus spending by the libraries fell from 4 per cent to 2.8 per cent during the 1980s. (For 'new' universities the decline has been from 5 per cent to 4 per cent.)

Just as important in promoting changes in the method of acquiring STM material has been the lack of library space available to house the traditional printed stock. The Follett committee dwelt in some length on this—in fact it was one of the points of departure for the Review itself.

In general all the university and many of the other research libraries have moved from a 'holdings' to an 'access' strategy in collection development. The distinction between collections being used for research and those supporting teaching and education has become less clear.

Supply (of information) in conflict with demand (library purchases)

A particularly revealing graph (Figure 22) shows the growth in university research in the USA (which closely correlates with the output of research articles) and the growth in library funding of the main 100 or so members of the Association of Research Libraries (ARL) in the USA. It implies a growing 'frustration gap' between the supply of published items in journal format and the ability of the libraries to keep pace with this growth.

What this graph shows is that the forces which generate the published research material are completely out of step with those which buy the material. The agencies which provide funds for research generation are often federal, with a commitment to the national good. The agencies which provide the library funds are totally separate. They are at a local level, library funding being finally decided upon by the financial officers of the institution within which the library sits. At this level there is a growing demand for funding from a variety of departments and subject areas, many of which can make a more convincing financial case for increased support. Gradually the library falls lower down the scale of priorities, and receives a diminishing proportion of the whole campus budget.

Figure 22: *US R&D and ARL library Expenditures (constant 1982 dollars)*

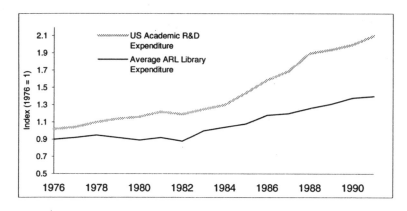

Sources: R&D: Science Engineering Indicators—1991, National Science Board. Library expenditure: Association of Research Libraries (ARL) Statistics.

It is this lack of coordination between the Supply and Demand forces which is at the heart of the disputes between publishers and librarians. Each group points to the other as the culprit in bringing the traditional STM information scene to chaos and imminent collapse. Yet the real culprit is the lack of balance between the two different information systems, the supply system (the authors) which is served by the publisher, and the demand system (the readers) which is served by the library.

The old concept of the author being also the reader and the STM information system being a closed loop is no longer valid. Authors have a different, more personal agenda. This agenda is to seek recognition and visibility from their peers and funding officers. This means that they need to publish to survive—'publish or perish' is as true in the 1990s as it was in the 1970s. The more they publish in respected, reputable and highly cited journals the more chance they stand of gaining promotion and a renewal of research support. This has sponsored such new features as 'salami publishing', and publishing of information which offers little new to the world of science, just to get more articles in print and in the *curriculum vitae*.

Many scientists have turned away from the printed journal system in the face of an 'information overload' with which they cannot cope. They constitute a group, referred to in a proprietary market research study undertaken by Harris Research on behalf of Mercury and the British Library Document Supply Centre (BLDSC), as the 'OINCS'—researchers who are 'out in the cold' as far as the mainstream of formal information dissemination is concerned. They form a substantial part of the total research community. They have turned their back on a print-based system which has failed to serve them well.

It is apparent that the old ways of publishing are no longer able to meet all the needs of the research community. Printed publishing of research material was adequate to those needs in the days of budgetary abundance, but in the 1990s we are forced to recognize the financial stresses within the system. The changing situation may be a dramatic stimulus to those new information systems which eliminate the inefficiencies of publishing for archive and exploit new communications media.

User studies on information behaviour

A further factor influencing the demand for printed and electronic information is the willingness of end users to adapt to both the old and the new forms of information. There are few studies which assess the social mechanisms of resistance or acceptance to media; the one's which have included such reviews have been revisited to see whether they have anything to say about future electronic information demand factors.

The Royal Society's Study on Scientific Information Systems

The Royal Society, in collaboration with several other information agencies, commissioned a study on the UK scientific information system in the early 1980s; this was followed by a further report coordinated by Professor Bryan Coles (Imperial College, London) during 1992/93 (Royal Society *et al.*, 1993). This second survey involved a detailed questionnaire being mailed to 4,356 researchers of which 2,398 (55 per cent) returned their completed forms.

As far as the spread of responses was concerned, biologists formed 32 per cent, engineers 19 per cent and mathematicians 14 per cent. Physicists were about 10 per cent.

The Royal Society results show that in 1992 more than 20 per cent of scientists were unaware of electronic bulletin boards and 76 per cent knew nothing of Adonis (an electronic document delivery service). In the UK the availability of an urgent action fax delivery service was often not advertised by the library for fear that the extra costs involved in using this special more expensive service would cripple their budget.

Only 20 per cent of users were prepared to fund the full cost of online searches, as a reflection of their preparedness to pay for information from their own pockets. Users in universities were less prepared than researchers in industry. There is also a difference between disciplines—engineers and biologists were more willing to pay costs of information than were physicists or mathematicians. Also, the younger scientists were less prepared to fund information services from their own pocket than older age groups.

All of which is disconcerting for those who would like to see a new source of funding enter the information business, with the personal funds of the individual being such a source. It appears that unless the main library budget breaks down in an uncontrolled way, the research scientists, particularly in academia (in the UK), will resist any attempt to switch the burden of funding from an institutional purse (the library) to an individual (themselves).

There was overwhelming support for print-on-paper versions of articles of interest delivered electronically (92 per cent). Reading on screen would be restricted to on screen scanning. A major concern of life-scientists was over the ability to reproduce 'images' on screen with sufficient clarity for close study.

The primacy of the research journal as the source for relevant research information came through strongly in the Royal Society survey. The newest technology-based sources were abstracts on CD-ROM, used by 10 per cent of the respondents. The low technology (printed journals and colleagues' communications) rate highly. Browsing is the most popular form of using the printed journal, whereby the contents of the journals were looked at first. Some of the older researchers browsed more generally, across a wider range of journals.

The Royal Society study indicated that overall—across all disciplines—50 per cent of users communicated with each other using e-mail. E-mail is used primarily for messages but also by some to distribute paper drafts to other authors.

Biologists, chemists and engineers were the most in favour of current awareness services, mathematicians the least. Those in the 26-35 age group were the most conservative. This may indicate a real resistance to change (or it may be lack of imagination on the benefits conferred by the new media).

In effect the Royal Society survey pointed to the conservatism of the research community in the UK and showed that although many new IT-based information services were available, in most cases the tried-and-tested printed form still reigned supreme. There was also a strong resistance to researchers paying for their information.

Study undertaken by D. Schauder, Australia

Don Schauder, Librarian at the Royal Melbourne Institute of Technology, has completed a similar thorough analysis of the role of the journal article in scientific communications (1994).

Besides the literature search into all aspects of the issue, Schauder also undertook some original market research using questionnaires. His findings indicated that the existing printed article system is what the research communities most want, and irresponsible attempts by other agencies to muscle into the electronic publishing of such items will do a great deal of disservice to science. It will heighten the already extensive tensions within the system.

Schauder used the responses he received from 582 academics in Australia, the UK and USA in a survey undertaken during the second half of 1992. The specific findings were:

- There is strong agreement on the importance of 'prestige' and 'size of readership' in selecting a journal for article submission. By quite a large margin 'speed in accepting and publishing articles' was seen to be of lesser importance.

- This 'prestige' aspect was translated into there being a positive feeling about the peer review system. Seventy-eight per cent of the respondents said peer review was 'important' and 16 per cent that it was of 'some importance' that the articles they personally submit for publication should be refereed before publication.

- The main negative concern about journal publishing is the high subscription price of such titles.

- A minority (39 per cent) reported that they were current users of national and international networks (1992). There were proportionately more network users from the biological sciences and medicine, followed by physical sciences and engineering; then social sciences, law and business; finally the arts. Of those who used the networks, 211 of 229 (92 per cent) used them primarily for electronic mail. 'Finding references to specific articles' was the next most popular use for the networks (14 per cent of returns).

- There was general satisfaction with document delivery services as used by librarians to get them their wanted articles.

- The great majority (more than 88 per cent) said they used their university library to meet their needs for journal subscriptions and individual articles.

- Eighty-two per cent of the respondents said that publishing professional articles was 'important' to their career advancement, while a further 14 per cent indicated that such publishing was of some importance to their careers.

- The respondents were ambivalent in their view on whether their university would give electronically published articles the same level of recognition as conventional journal articles for academic award/promotion. Thirty-three per cent did not feel competent to answer this question.

In summary, the Schauder study supports the continuance of the existing print-based journal article publishing system, whilst also pointing out that there were tensions inherent within STM which were threatening to come to a head as electronic publishing gains apace.

User studies undertaken by Loughborough University

Professor Jack Meadows has coordinated a number of studies over time to establish how researchers reacted to the availability of electronic information systems. In particular he has collected data on the variations in computer usage by UK scientists from the mid 1980s to early 1990s (Bukhari and Meadows, 1992). The most striking point is the growth in usage of networked services, reflecting a rapid uptake due to improved networking in the UK during this period.

Figure 23: *Use of electronic and networked information services in UK academia*

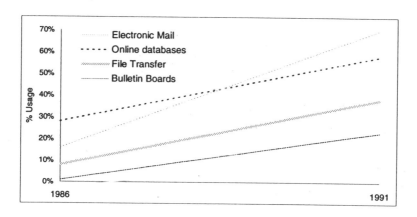

Loughborough University has also recently completed a study on the use of networked information by biologists in the UK (Meadows, 1994). Two universities, a government research centre and a pharmaceutical company were surveyed for their use of biological information sources. This study showed that although there were substantial networked facilities—notably e-mail and bulletin boards—among biologists this was far from universal. The biologists in the pharmaceutical companies made considerably more use of such facilities than did biologists in other institutions.

The reasons for the lack of total commitment to electronic information services is only partly due to the existence (or non-existence) of facilities. It is also whether the researchers knew of the availability of the networked information service (something which emerged from the Royal Society report), and also whether force of habit kept many researchers to the old, well-tried printed information systems.

Figure 24: *Percentage of biologists using networked information services*

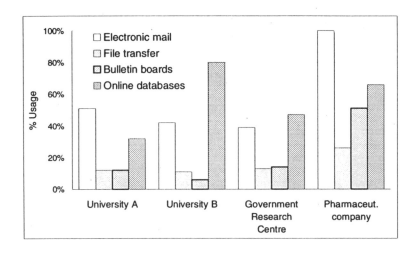

Professor Meadows comments that a transfer of activity from print or speech to electronic forms can affect accepted boundaries between traditional methods of communication. Electronic information changes the paradigm to something which may have little comparison with that which it replaced. The distinction, so apparent in printed publishing, between formal and informal systems (communication and exchange of initial research findings, compared with the refereed article) might not be so apparent in the electronic information system. There are some electronic services on the Internet which, within the one system, allow the full range of information exchange from letters, file transfers, editorial information, conference/meeting summaries, advertising, and a moderated bulletin board. It is a short leap from here to the full electronic journal.

A limitation to the growth in electronic journals is the existing system of reward to researchers. Formal publications in quality journals are an essential part of the researcher's *curriculum vitae*. Their number and quality determine the success of a researcher's career. Therefore, will the academic assessment process accept electronic publications on a par with printed publications?

Speed—the key component of the electronic publication—is not the highest priority for researchers (in academia) according to Schauder's recent study (1994). Prestige is more important, and electronic journals are considered low under this criterion.

Figure 25*: Important factors in selecting a journal for publication*

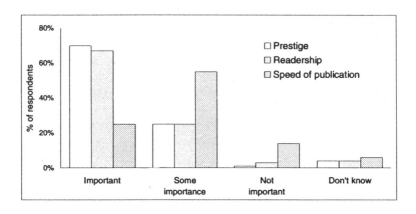

As Professor Meadows demonstrates, the electronic infrastructure for networked communications is not universally available. Not all researchers are able to access the electronic journal, and having accessed it, want to read it on the screen. Add to this the fact that such specialized electronic journals, carrying quality information, are likely to become more expensive to create and support (particularly if the international networks are forced into some form of cost recovery), then the willingness by organizations to produce 'electronic journals' may remain hobbyist rather than commercial in motivation, amateur rather than professional in approach.

Survey undertaken by Strathclyde University

Liz Davenport, then at Strathclyde University, (now at Queen Margaret College, Edinburgh), spent the period between January and June 1992 interviewing a wide range of practitioners in the information industry to establish whether any consensus was emerging over the application of new media to information dissemination. An analysis was made of the transcripts which were made during these interviews (Davenport, 1994). The researchers showed little awareness of the structural changes taking place in electronic publishing. Few were involved with the economic decisions which were being made to balance the collection development budgets within their libraries. Many were beginning to come to terms with 'free at the point of usage' for their required published material. None admitted to paying the top-up for essential publications. The library exists, in their opinion, to minimize their involvement in publication acquisition. The erosion of the central library budget was something few of Ms Davenport's interviewees were really aware of.

On the other hand, publishers at that time (1992) showed a preoccupation with document delivery. The prices which several publishers were thinking of instituting displayed a wide range. They were consistent in being above the price level expectation of the researchers and librarians.

Not unexpectedly, librarians focused on pricing as a major issue.

The Faxon Institute Studies

This market survey was perhaps the first professional approach taken to understanding the changing needs for information by end users. It used a number of psychologists to investigate end user behaviour through observation techniques, and by inviting the researchers they were studying to keep diaries and complete questionnaires (Almquist, 1991).

Two studies were undertaken; the first involved three subject areas in 1991, and the second more in-depth study of two further subjects in 1992. The results from both these studies tended to be subject-specific. These identified great differences in information collection patterns between the various key disciplines.

The subjects in 1991 were chemistry, genetics and computer science. In 1992 the study turned its attention to radio astronomers and biologists. However, one key conclusion was that researchers were not the same with respect to their information collection needs. There were distinct 'groups', which in the first of the Faxon Institute studies were as follows:

Information Zealots	24 per cent
Classic Scientists	25 per cent
Young Technologists	12 per cent

Information Anxious	16 per cent
Older Teachers	10 per cent
Product Researchers	13 per cent

The 'Information Anxious' group occurs in a number of guises. They were identified in a recent extensive study commissioned by Mercury Enterprises as 'OINCS' (Out IN the Cold), as tending to reject conventional and new information systems. They have turned their backs on publications as a source for ideas and results, either because they could be obtained more easily from less formal sources, or because there was a barrier to their use. They represent 50 per cent of the user base within UK industry.

A corollary to the above is the self-perception of information 'competency' among the 600 or so researchers analyzed by the Faxon Institute. One third of the respondents felt that they read less than 20 per cent of what they needed to in order to do their job well. Only 27 per cent felt they read more than half of what was required.

One other relevant background factor of interest is the perception of usefulness of the various information modes by researchers along with actual usage. For example, during the week prior to the study the researchers indicated that the following were the frequency of usage of different media types: Electronic mail (14.7), personal/library files (9.7), telephone conversations (9.5), personal discussions (7.7). The library was well down (2.8) as was fax (2.6) and CD-ROM.

The CORE Chemical Researchers User Study

The CORE project at Cornell University has been underway for some four to five years. It has involved the participation of several organizations, each contributing their respective expertise and facilities: BellCore offered their technical know-how; the Online Computer Library Center (OCLC) provided software development tools; the American Chemical Society (ACS) contributed a stable of over 20 primary research journals; and CAS (Chemical Abstracts Service) supplied the bibliographic database. The Mann Library at Cornell University provided the infrastructure and the access path to the research chemists on campus at Ithica. CORE is an attempt to develop an electronic publishing system for chemistry researchers which marries text with graphics in delivering data within a network.

The original aim was to come up with conclusions after two years of research. In fact, the extent of the problems which they faced were such as to make the project a much lengthier one. The starting point was to develop a system which overcame reliance on purely textual information. It was felt that this was the reason for the poor response to the Chemical Journals Online project (which offered full text of ACS and other chemical publishers' journals). Integrating images was seen to offer better value to the researcher.

The Mann Library staff conducted an extensive survey of users, not only chemists but also physical and social scientists, to establish a benchmark journal usage pattern. The system was then built using the expertise from BellCore and OCLC. More recently the Mann Library staff have been repeating their usage studies to see how the system as delivered met with the expectations of users.

Chemists have an indispensable need for information. However, there are different types of information and various ways of getting it. Printed matter, rather than computer-generated sources, is used for 'keeping up to date'. Retrospective literature searching is carried out with the aid of computers, however. If a specific name or fact is being sought the computer would again prove useful. Chemists at Cornell tend to go to libraries about once per week. Some scholars, particularly those who find the library geographically inconvenient, have taken out personal subscriptions to a few key journals.

Another finding from the ongoing CORE market research is that chemists do not read an article from start to finish (unless it is exactly in their area of interests). Once they find a potentially relevant article they skip from the abstract to the figures, to the conclusion. They also demand access to older material, which cannot be found in the last five years of the experimental database. Having gained access to a relevant article, they then photocopy it and file it in their personal filing systems. These are usually unstructured, so that retrieval of the copied article is often from memory rather than with the help of a sophisticated local access procedure.

The chemists at Cornell had high expectations of the electronic system which, by and large, were not met. They wanted:

- graphics rather than bibliographic text files
- information presented clearly on the screen
- local printout facility
- a graphic searching software package (based on pattern matching)

- the ability to flip through all the scanned images of graphics, without getting lost
- a system which encourages serendipity

In the event, CORE was a disappointment in the early days. It was found that, however good the online interface, for serendipity the user preferred hard copy to the online system. 'The machine takes thought away from me', was a disheartened cry from one of the chemists.

The CORE results again showed that there is no uniformity in the way researchers search for new information. They are more graphic-orientated, and they will only scan electronic information if there is a plentiful supply of 'thumbnails' within the document which allow them to see in summary form what the article is about.

Royal Society of Chemistry Study on Users

Dr Ivor Williams (1993) from the Royal Society of Chemistry has reported on his recent market research which showed the limited use being made by research chemists in the UK of chemical journal titles available in an online format.

Three hundred copies of a questionnaire were mailed to chemical researchers in universities in the UK. Their use of certain categories of chemical journals are as follows.

In chemistry the use of secondary literature is widespread. In fact, 86 of the 97 respondents claimed to be 'regular' users of at least one secondary service (*Chemical Abstracts* being predominant). There was a low level of usage of *Chemical Journals Online*, which is believed to be due to the absence of structural formulae, other illustrations and tabular matter.

Most of the respondents had made use of online searches, though only 37 of the 73 had conducted such a search themselves. Twenty-seven had used CD-ROM. Research chemists are familiar with electronic information services, so it is surprising to find from Dr Williams' study that only 100 of 1,100 papers reported as being 'used' were identified from online database searches.

Ninety per cent of papers were found from what was defined as 'low tech' sources. The traditional journal is more relevant as a source for information. Chemists overall make use of 11-12 journal titles in their research, though this does vary by discipline. Colleagues and hard copy abstracts are relevant. This reliance on traditional methods may be due to technophobia, but equally may be a reflection of the entrenched conservatism in the way people search for information. A social revolution may be required before this changes. Dr Williams suggests that research chemists know which journals are relevant for their purposes, and by browsing through these channels they are able to keep up to date in their own particular fields in a comprehensive and fairly painless way. The following figure summarizes Dr William's analysis of where research chemists find the papers they use.

Figure 26: *Access to papers of interest to UK chemists*

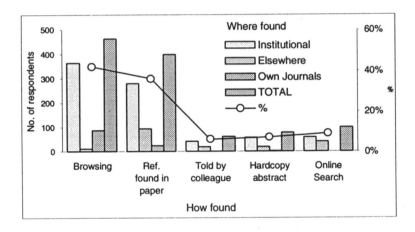

Respondents in the 20-29 age group were less enthusiastic about 'browsing' through traditional sources than the older groups (7.8 journals on average, with only 27 per cent of papers used being reported as found this way). Inorganic chemists browse more than the younger researchers (39 per cent) and among more titles (9.8 journals) but still less than the research chemists on average. Organic chemists, by comparison, found 52 per cent of their papers from browsing, this time among 15 journals on average.

Dr Williams' results suggest that a reduction in the number of journal titles—the basis of much of the research dissemination in chemistry—would not serve the best interests of the community. Fewer titles would mean less access to browsing.

Secondary services, online searching, is essentially a back-stop activity. Only 10 per cent of the activity is in this area.

The electronic journal, *Chemical Journals Online*, fulfils a set of functions and purposes of its own and is not comparable to the printed journals. It is still the printed journal, available in the main research libraries, which is the focus for research effort.

Conclusions

These various studies illustrate one almost consistent theme—that both existing and new information systems fail to excite users. They will need to be enticed away from their general apathy (about 20-50 per cent of researchers) or from their commitment to the well-tried and tested print-based systems. The added value generated by the new systems must be sufficiently great as to make such changes in habit worthwhile.

Technology

Barriers to new media

There is a variety of restrictions preventing full and open access to the electronic publications currently being made available. Some of these are administrative (the role of copyright protection will be discussed later). Some are socio/technical, with many software and display interfaces, information retrieval languages and database structures inappropriate to users' needs (see above). This implies the development of expensive, multidisciplinary technologies which are beyond the scope of most existing players (*IMO Reviews*).

Nevertheless, technology will come to the rescue in some instances. Enhancements will be developed as researchers improve the hardware and software systems currently available, and, by taking greater account of the needs of end users, some of the earlier resistance to new information systems may be dispelled. The implication is that the new media systems will require much greater involvement by the IT experts to make them more 'user friendly' and therefore acceptable.

Improvements in software and hardware

In a recent report initially made available as an electronic publication, free on the Internet, Andrew Odlyzko from AT&T Bell Laboratories describes some of the more immediate technical advances which are occurring (1995). As the benchmark he comments on the historical development whereby information has doubled every fifteen years (see later) or about 7 per cent per annum. This pales into insignificance in comparison with the doubling in speed of microprocessors which is happening every eighteen months (or 60 per cent per annum growth). Communication speeds are also making rapid progress. The packets switched through the Internet grew by a factor of 128 during the period 1988 to 1991, whereas the costs of sustaining the network rose only 68 per cent.

Odlyzko also comments on the fact that storage of information in digital form may have been a limitation to electronic information in the past. All the mathematics papers currently being published, both in journal and book form, would account for a storage requirement of 4 Gbytes. A 9 Gbyte magnetic disc cost (in 1994) about £2,000 in the US, and a write-once 7 Gbyte optical disc about £200 (though the associated write-to hardware is still expensive). Digital tapes may be even cheaper and will be available soon with capacities of 250 Gbytes. The point is that it is already possible to store all the world's key mathematics information in digital form at a cost of less than one of the core journal subscriptions.

Software has been referred to as a limitation. In the future, technology will allow even more scholars to do their own typesetting. TeX has been widely adopted by researchers in the physics and mathematics-related areas, and also by publishers who have been forced to adopt such input systems in the name of keeping costs down. The search and retrieval interfaces have been thrown into turmoil by the popularity of the Mosaic interface within the World Wide Web on the Internet. Mosaic may be the 'killer application' for the Internet, though even without Mosaic the growth in usage has been dramatic (see later).

In effect, technology is creating the basis for a new paradigm in scholarly information transfer. No longer constrained to a process which relies on the printed page, new electronic opportunities are opening up every few months as users of the emerging information technology seek to make it a servant of the information dissemination process.

The following table sets out some of the many and various expected changes which will occur between 1992 and the year 2000 in the available technology.

Table 6: Relevant technology trends

1992	2000
Computer power 50 times cheaper than 1982	Portable CD-ROM based information devices at 20% of today's prices
Display 14", 256 colour screens at £400	HDTV resolution, thousands of colours £200 equivalent
CD-ROM drives 1 million worldwide (£200 per unit)	60 million drives (half in homes) at £60 per unit
Floppy discs Store 180 pages of text	Store 2,400 pages of text
Power consumption High/medium power requirement	Low power consumption
Telecom modems 30 pages/minute transmission	120 pages/minute. Also ISDN capability
User Interaction Keyboard, but increasingly graphic interface	Keyboarding, graphical, touch screen, voice recognition
Documentation Printed manuals	Documentation and help functions on CD-ROM
Databases Text	Text, image and sound databases
Storage Analogue predominates Cost of storage £3/Mb	Digital capture, storage, reproduction and dissemination. Cost £0.30/Mb
Media Solutions Isolated	Integrated, hybrid solutions: hard disc, CD-ROM and online processing
Archives Paper, microfiche	Optical discs

Source: Information Workstation Group, Consulting Trust GmbH

All these changes will have an impact on the development of new media. They will provide the infrastructure on which new information players will build to produce new packages of scholarly data. A question which is confronting print-based publishers is what part they will play in the migration from print to electronic information systems. Will publishers gain the same strong position in electronic publishing as they have in print-based systems? According to the Consulting Trust GmbH, in a report undertaken for the European Commission (1993), the likelihood of this is low. There are a number of reasons proposed for the potential 'disappearance' of the traditional print-based publisher:

- The content they hold is only part of future multimedia publishing needs

- They have only limited know-how and skills for developing the new media products of the future

- The traditional editorial experience is a barrier to electronic publishing

- They are not used to 'publishing on demand' (at the article or document level)

Technical infrastructure

There is a chicken and egg syndrome affecting new information systems. Producers will not create products for a new system unless there are strong indications that the associated hardware and software systems— the infrastructure—are in place. After all, the investment needed to create the product will only make commercial sense if there are enough outlets in place to ensure that the investment costs are recouped together with an acceptable 'surplus'.

The early 1990s were only just witnessing the emergence of sufficient hardware platforms on which to play the new media. There are some 100 million personal computers (PCs) worldwide, of which 90 per cent are IBM compatible and 10 per cent are Apple Mac. These PCs are only now beginning to penetrate the office, with 35 per cent of US and 25 per cent of European offices having PCs. The penetration of PCs in the home is 20 per cent in the USA and 15 per cent in Europe.

CD-ROM readers are also more in evidence. There are an estimated one million in total worldwide (see Table 6); 75 per cent of these are PC-related, while 15 per cent are attached to Apple Mac systems and 10 per cent are either Unix-related, CD-I or Datadiscman. The networks are also a driving force in the move towards new media adoption. The Internet has seen a remarkable growth, with over 30 million users. Policy decisions by governments in the USA and Europe to create 'digital superhighways' are also promoting a new awareness of the sorts of material which could be fed through these powerful communication channels.

The integration of images, moving images, and sound with data and text to create multimedia information products is also a stimulus for change. These products can be accommodated on CD-ROM players and on CD-I platforms, and will increasingly be fed through the superhighway networks. The value-added element offered by such multi-sensory approaches to information packaging and dissemination is encouraging a new group of players to enter the market, players who have hitherto been active in the film and television studios, or within computer software houses. They are more able to adapt to the technological challenges of bringing a product to market within a high-tech environment.

Changes are inevitable in the structure of the information industry in the UK by the year 2003. The changes are driven partly by market forces, which are increasingly antagonistic towards the old formula of printed subscription products; partly by the technology which allows a new technical infrastructure to be put in place within the user community; and partly by the new players who are beginning to see a commercial opportunity in the new information media.

The factors influencing change are combining to create a new scholarly publishing paradigm by the year 2003. Within this framework the printed book and journal will undoubtedly have a place, but the appeal of new and more efficient information systems, relying on computers, optical storage and telecommunications, will become more evident and acceptable.

Conclusions

This section has explored some of the background factors which will influence the ability of the market as users to acquire scholarly information in future. The picture is not conducive to supporting any sense of optimism. There are few social and economic indicators which would lead one to assume that the Demand sector for information will return to the halcyon days of the early 1970s. There are too many other social missions which compete with research for a limited public purse; there is a growing emphasis on education rather than high level research within the academic sector; and what research is being conducted is increasingly focused on producing near-term market applications.

At the same time there is a large infrastructure in existence which will maintain some ongoing momentum for the current information system. Social habits die hard, and those brought up with the printed book and journal may take longer to change their habits than the technology allows. Conservatism is a key feature of the scholarly information system which sees the reward to researchers not primarily in any commercial sense but more in terms of such undying features as 'prestige', 'esteem' and 'recognition'. Such motives are not easily transferred to the electronic publishing environment.

References

Almquist, E. (1991) *An examination of work-related information acquisition and usage among scientific, technical and medical fields.* The 1991 Faxon Institute Annual Conference, Reston, VA, April 1991.

Bukhari, A.A. and Meadows, A.J. (1992) The use of information technology by scientists in British and Saudi Arabian universities: a comparative study. *Journal of Information Science*, **18**, 409-415.

Consulting Trust GmbH (1993) *New Opportunities for Publishers in the Information Services Market*, EUR 14925 EN, January 1993.

Davenport, E. (1994) Perception of economics in a digital publishing environment. A report of a field study. *Interlending and Document Supply*, **22**(4), 8-16.

East, H. (1991) *Balancing the books: resourcing electronic information services in academic and public libraries.* CCIS Policy Paper 3; British Library R&D Report 6057. London: Centre for Communication and Information Studies.

East, H. and Tilson, Y. (1993) *The liberated enduser: developments in practice and policy for database provision to the academic community.* CCIS Policy Paper No. 4, July 1993. London: University of Westminster.

Follett Review (1993) *Joint Funding Councils' Libraries Review Group: Report*. (Chairman: Sir Brian Follett). Bristol: HEFCE.

IMO Reviews. Information Market Observatory (IMO), Reports on specific new media developments in Europe. EU DG13, Luxembourg.

Martyn, J., Vickers, P., and Feeney, M. (eds.) (1990) *Information UK 2000*. London: Bowker Saur.

Meadows, A.J. (1994) Is the future beginning to work? Academics and networks. In *Changing patterns of online information: UKOLUG State of the Art Conference 1994*, Edinburgh.

Odlyzko, A. (1995) Tragic loss or good riddance? The impending demise of traditional scholarly journals. *International Journal of Human-Computer Studies* (in press). Condensed version in *Notices of the American Mathematical Society*, January 1995. Available from ftp://netlib.att.com/netlib/att.math.odlyzko/tragic.loss

Royal Society, British Library and Association of Learned and Professional Society Publishers (1993) *The scientific, technical and medical information system in the UK*. British Library R&D Report 6123. London: The Royal Society.

Schauder, D. (1994) Electronic publishing of professional articles: attitudes of academics and implications for the scholarly communication industry. *Journal of the American Society for Information Science*, **45**(2), 3-100.

Unesco (1993) *World Science Report*. Paris: Unesco Publishing.

Williams, I.A. (1993) How chemists use the literature. *Learned Publishing*, **6**(2), April.

SECTION C

Supply-side Economics

*I don't believe in publishers who wish to butter their
bannocks on both sides while they'll hardly allow an
author to smell treacle. I consider they are too grabby
together and like Methodists they love to keep the
Sabbath and everything else they can lay their hands on.*
Amanda Ros, to Lord Ponsonby, 1910.

THE PRESENT SCHOLARLY PUBLISHING SYSTEM

Fragmentation within publishing

The average European information provider is smaller, less vertically
integrated, and much more nationally oriented than its US counterpart.
More 'convergence' between technology areas is occurring in the USA
and Japan as compared with Europe (*IMO Review*). A reflection of the
diversity of the journal publishing industry is shown in Table 7 (Brown,
1993).

This table shows the decentralization, or fragmentation, of the publishing industry. It suggests that the 'typical' scientific journal publisher
is not like Elsevier, Springer, Wiley or Academic Press, but is the small,
sometimes hobbyist, publisher producing a journal from his office or
home with limited resources. There are over 16,000 such publishers on
B.H. Blackwell's list of active publishers, and even this may not represent the full total, bearing in mind that the British Library Document
Supply Centre acquires 48,000 serial titles each year. Small, cottage
industry publishing prevails in the global scholarly publishing world;
Elsevier, the market leader, controls at best only 15 per cent of journal

publication output.

Table 7: *Fragmentation of worldwide journal publishing*

Size of Publisher (as reflected in their turnover with B.H. Blackwell, subscription agency)	Number of Publishers	Number of Titles
Publishers with a turnover in excess of £50,000	117	7,086
Publishers with a turnover between £5,000 and £50,000	987	4,047
Publishers with a turnover of less than £5,000	16,427	23,700
Total	**17,531**	**34,833**

Source: Personal communication, J. Cox, B.H. Blackwell, March 1992

Economies of scale

This fragmentation and the predominance of small scale operators will influence the form which electronic publishing may take by the year 2003. On the basis that the new media require an investment in, if not understanding of, electronic and optical publishing systems, it is only the largest publishers which have the reserves to plough into building up such expertise. There is an 'economy of scale' which is small for a printed publication programme. The economy of scale is larger for an organization which uses information technology to deliver its publications. It is an indication of the problems facing the publishing industry in coming to terms with the challenge of new media that the pioneers and market leaders are organizations which come from outside the traditional STM publishing business. They do not have the same learning curve to follow in understanding the intricacies of new media publishing.

'Industry convergence'

A key factor is the emergence of partnerships between publishers, on the one hand, and hardware/software and telecommunications organizations on the other. Examples of such relationships include:

- BellCoRe with the American Chemical Society, CAS and OCLC at Cornell University in *Chemistry Online Retrieval Experiment* (CORE), available through the Mann Library to the Cornell University campus.

- OCLC with its *OCLC Online Journals* is offering publishers the ability to make their journals available through their GUIDON software interface, distributed through their network of 18,000 libraries worldwide and, if necessary, converted to an industry standard text-tagging system—Standard Generalized Markup Language (SGML)—through their in-house processing unit. A number of UK and European publishers are making use of aspects of the OCLC menu, including Chapman and Hall, Institute of Electrical Engineers, Current Science and Elsevier Trend Journals (Cambridge). More recently Elsevier has announced that all its 1,100 journals will be made available though OCLC.

- AT&T with Springer (plus others) and University of California at San Francisco in the *Red Sage* project. This is now being extended by AT&T into a formal business venture and will seek publisher support for a comprehensive online journal experiment in the biosciences area.

- Institute for Scientific Information (ISI) and IBM are creating an *ISI Electronic Library* using IBM's technical expertise and ISI's ability to bring over 1,000 full text biomedical and life science journals into the system.

- Microsoft with Dorling Kindersley, whereby the former has an equity share in the latter and will be using its high technology experience to repackage D-K's extensive catalogue of books in a multimedia form.

- Adobe (Acrobat) with Wiley and Chapman and Hall in the *CD-ROM Acrobat Journals Using Networks* (CAJUN) project.

- Holzenbrink (Germany) with Voyager (USA) and Macmillan.

An increasing number of such cross-fertilization projects in the information industry sector are anticipated to take advantage of the synergy from the respective cultures—publishing and technical—which can be applied to information problems in the STM area.

The emergence of such new players is nevertheless causing considerable concern in many sectors of traditional publishing. Publishers fear that they will dictate unacceptable terms by virtue of controlling the distribution of electronic products to the market. While publishers controlled the channels to end users they could dictate terms to bookshops and subscription agents. They are comparatively powerless in the electronic environment and, with the new interest in the STM area from AT&T, Mercury, SURFnet and others, paranoia is rising.

Ownership of publication rights

This is the main current defence mechanism for publishers.

Since scientific work results in outputs that may be protected by intellectual property rights, issues of freedom of information, particularly the rights of free discussion of scientific issues and unrestricted access to scientific information, are coming io the fore. At the same time, complaints about 'price gouging'—publishers increasing the prices of journal subscriptions at levels far in excess of inflationary rates in general—have triggered a move towards denying electronic rights to publishers and their retention by academic institutions, the funding agencies or even the authors themselves.

The ownership of electronic rights, and the impact which this will have on the industry, is one of the critical issues to emerge. If universities and funding agencies continue the trend of holding on to these rights, then the ability to secure the widespread physical dissemination of published information would appear greater than if commercial publishers retain their present hold over both printed and electronic copyright.

The rights ownership issue is also relevant in a national perspective. The USA is particularly interested in this issue, and a recent study undertaken on behalf of the American Association of University Presidents included it as a major part of their investigation into the future of information systems on university campuses (Association of American Universities, 1994). Other countries are perhaps less excited about this issue, although in the UK the Follett Review (1993) made reference to the need for pilot experiments between universities and publishers to reach amicable settlements on what it sees as an increasingly emotive issue.

Geographical distribution of publications

Figure 27 shows which countries are significant as producers of research publications.

***Figure 27**: Scientific production (publications) in different areas of the world*

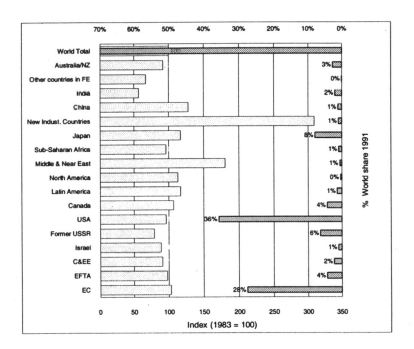

Source: Science Citation Index and OST

While there have been disputes in the past concerning simultaneous discovery, controversies and legal wrangles on priorities are much more common today. These, and commercial as well as strategic and defence interests, are leading to secrecy rather than openness in science. Hoaxes, plagiarism and reluctance to acknowledge original sources are being reported in the press, and public investigations are becoming an unfortunate feature of the scientific scene.

, GROWTH IN OUTPUT OF INFORMATION

In overall terms there has been a long and sustained growth in the number of new titles, both books and journals, available to the research community. The number of scientific papers published annually has been doubling every 10-15 years for the last two centuries (de Solla Price, 1963). There are several reasons for this.

The 'twigging phenomenon'

History has shown that the increase in the rate of information growth is not a new phenomenon. Derek de Solla Price, in his classic study *Little Science, Big Science*, plotted the growth in new journal title releases as shown in Figure 28.

In effect, the number of journal titles has expanded every year, doubling every 15 years. In 1980 there were 62,000 titles listed in *Ulrich's International Periodicals Directory* (Bowker) and in 1992 126,000. It should be pointed out that the latter figure did include the Irregular Serials which were not part of the former number. But even so, there has been continued growth in published output.

What has produced this expansion? It is not just the productivity of the researchers themselves—after all, these could have been contained within the 'core' journal publishing system. The output of new journals is a product of the nature of science itself. It is the 'twigging phenomenon'. Science progresses by pushing back the barriers to knowledge at the periphery of each subject area. As more and more researchers concentrate on specific parts of the science periphery, so the need for a formal mechanism for information interchange arises. This then promotes the production of a journal for the new research area. The journal acts as the catalyst; it formalizes the exchange of research information within that particular research area. It legitimizes the speciality. This social need has helped to create the expansion in titles. Figure 29 shows how this relates to the 'twigging' of science.

Another (slightly misleading) graph, which is used to show the growth

Figure 28: *Total number of scientific journals and abstract journals founded as a function of date*

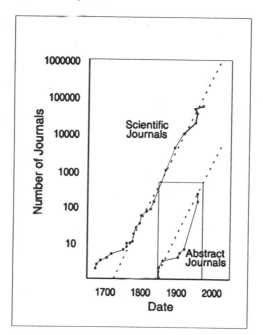

Source: *Little Science, Big Science*, Derek de Solla Price, Columbia University Press, 1963

in journal titles, is reproduced from *Ulrich's International Periodical Directory* (Figure 30).

This is misleading in that it takes no account of the change in Bowker's (the publisher of the Directory) selection criterion for inclusion in the Directory, which prevents a true extrapolation of serial title launches. The *LA Record* (February 1994) suggests that the above table ignores the fact that between 1987 and 1992/3 Ulrich's increasingly brought Irregular Serials into the main database, which accounted for an extra 36,000 titles.

Figure 29: The tree of journal publishing development

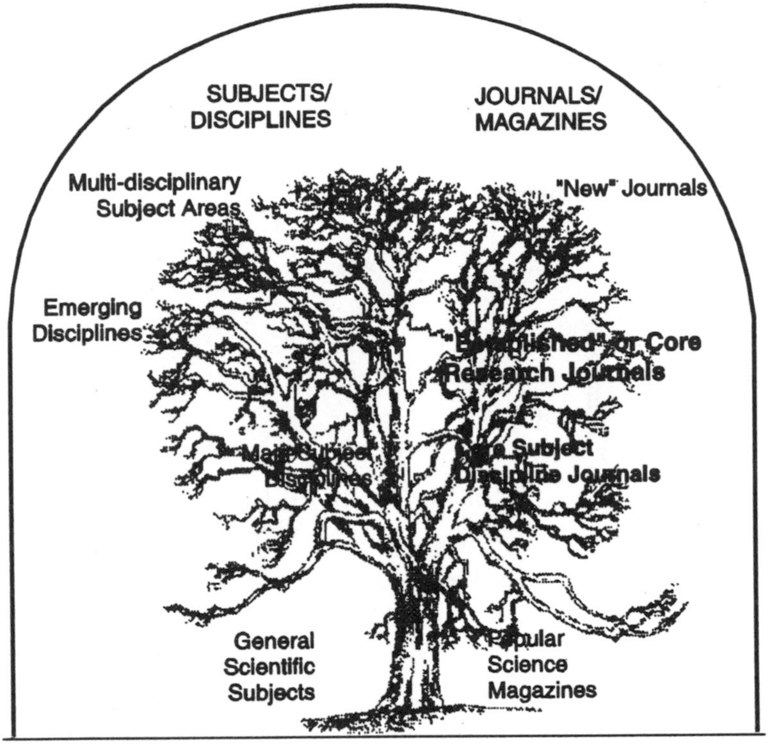

Motivation

Critical to the information problem, as we now perceive it, is an understanding of the mechanisms which drive researchers to publish. 'Publish or perish' is perhaps a cliché but accurate nonetheless.

Researchers need to see their results in print, in order to guarantee tenure, enhance their reputation in their peer group, secure financial support from the funding bodies, obtain promotion, and so on. The results, with increased pressure for limited R&D funds, have meant that information availability has grown out of synch with the (nationally-determined) academic library budgets (see Section B above).

A widening gap has therefore emerged between supply and demand

Figure 30: Growth of journal titles

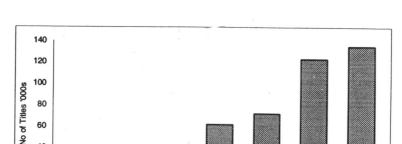

Source: *Ulrich's International Periodical Directory*

capabilities in the academic and research information sectors. The output is growing, sustained by issues which are unrelated to market funding mechanisms.

THE INFORMATION INDUSTRY OVERALL

Information industry market size

As a backdrop to this analysis, the following section provides a brief assessment of the relative size of the information industry components, both geographically and in terms of product/service mix.

Figure 31, a summary table from the Consulting Trust study commissioned by the European Commission (1993), shows where the European information industry fits in with its US and Japanese competitors.

The strength of the USA in the R&D sector, the software and computing area, and notably in electronic information services, is a source of concern to the European Commission as well as partly explaining why many new electronic information services originate and mature on the other side of the Atlantic.

Figure 31: *Information industry ratio comparison*

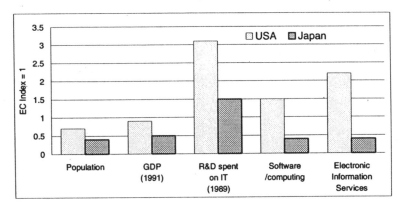

Source: Consulting Trust GmbH

More particularly, the *US Industrial Outlook* data (Figure 32) show that the emergence of electronic information services has been as recent as it has been dramatic. From a business which hardly existed seven years

Figure 32: *Value of different media in the USA (in $ bil)*

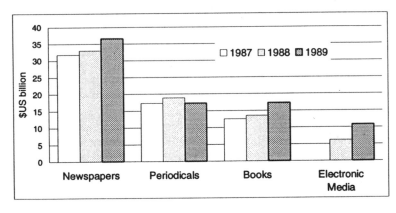

Source: *US Industrial Outlook*

ago, it now competes in size with periodicals and books for a slice of the overall information industry in the USA.

Electronic media

The European Community's information services sector (telecomms, software, computing, and online/off-line products) totalled 135 BECU in 1991 (£95 bil); of this telecomms accounted for 80 BECU (£56 bil), and software and computing for 55 BECU (£38 bil) of which electronic information services contributed 55 per cent (or 3.1 BECU/£2.2 bil).

An estimation of the international electronic information services sector is shown in Figure 33.

Figure 33: Industry turnover in BECU (online and off-line)

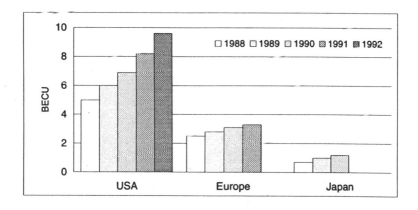

Source: *US Industrial Outlook*

The above evidence shows that the electronic information industry already has a considerable presence, albeit more entrenched in some pockets of the business than in others. Those sectors where there is a need for immediate information—such as the financial and business sectors—have moved completely to the electronic delivery systems at the expense of print. STM information has not made such a dramatic transition.

Print media

In comparison, the European print publishing sector was worth 75.5 BECU (£52.8 billion) in 1991 (source: Consulting Trust GmbH). This was broken down into the following main categories:

newspapers	25%
magazines	22%
books	18.5%
corporate	10%

An estimation of the sizes of the international print publishing markets in 1990 and 1995 are shown in Table 8.

Table 8: International print publishing markets

	1990	1995	Growth
Europe (EC)	17.1 BECU	19.8 BECU	16%
USA	16.5 BECU	18.0 BECU	10%
Japan	4.6 BECU	4.9 BECU	6%

Professional publishing in print amounts to 25 BECU or £17 billion (1991). The equivalent electronic information sector is 3.3 BECU or £2.3 billion (1991). This shows that print still dominates within the professions.

Growth in printed publishing in Europe has been 3.8 per cent per annum in the past ten years. Growth in electronic information has been 15-20 per cent per annum (Consulting Trust GmbH, 1993).

PRINTED PUBLICATIONS

Background

A key factor affecting the strength of the printed publication system would be the introduction of a requirement to submit grant applications to potential sponsors in electronic rather than printed format. When such grant applications are the norm, and when tenure, promotion and peer-group prestige are awarded on the basis of electronic publications, then the future for printed books and journals becomes bleak.

It is also evident that many information providers are using electronic production systems to create 'publications', and whether these are produced in printed or electronic format is essentially dictated by market judgements rather than technical constraints.

The SGML issue

Electronic publishing is moving into two areas. The first is the delivery of new media products using the various optical and electronic procedures available. These will be commented on in following sections.

The other area is the in-house organization of information into structured files. It is only in the past five years that there has been an international standard—ISO 8868 Standard Generalized Markup Language (SGML)—which covers this. In effect this produces a 'neutral' database from which, with the judicious application of codes and protocols to the structured file, a variety of output formats are possible, including typeset and printed versions.

Though SGML is seen to be of immense value to publishers it is only in the past year or so that the larger STM publishers have followed this particular path. The reason is that whilst SGML exists in a general form it does not cover some of the scientific material in journal articles—for example, chemical compounds, complex mathematics, tables and graphs. Some of these issues are being addressed; partly through putting these items into a separate TIFF (Tagged Image File Format) or EPS (Encapsulated PostScript) file with pointers; and partly through further enhancements to the SGML ISO coding. A new ISO standard giving enhancements has been published (April 1994) as ISO 12083, and this goes into more depth in the tagging of full text mathematical tables, etc. However, it still does not meet the needs of *all* STM material.

The implication is that SGML offers an efficient road into electronic publishing (EP) for publishers. Its neutrality takes away the need for publishers to predict the market demand for any one electronic delivery option. A single database can spin off, on demand, a variety of EP products.

There is, however, a price to pay. There is an up-front cost in developing the required software to run SGML in-house, including the editor software, the parsers to provide automatic correction of the material, and the database management system within which to store the electronic files. It is also necessary to develop a document type definition (DTD), the set of rules which govern the implementation of SGML in a real world environment. Having incurred these costs, the publisher will then increase his operational costs as he applies tags to each article item to provide the common tagging structure.

Some of the larger STM publishers are strongly committed to the SGML process. Elsevier embarked on a programme of keying in the header files of its entire journal publishing programme—1,100 titles—some five years ago. It had to write its own DTD for these article headers. Approximately half the Elsevier journals are now being processed through this CAP-CAS (Computer Aided Production, leading to Current Awareness Services) system. Meanwhile, Springer Verlag and Kluwer Academic joined forces with some European centres to create an alternative header DTD known as MAJOUR. Both these DTDs are available to the STM publishing community.

The full text of the article in SGML is taking longer to develop because of the complex mathematics, symbols and non-standard character sets which are a feature of scientific publishing. Very few examples exist of such STM titles being processed in this way, though we should see some developments soon.

Many other publishers are beginning to stir in this area. Several have written their own DTDs and others are linking themselves to the Elsevier or MAJOUR system. Progress is relatively slow, partly because of the investment required from companies which are considerably smaller in size than Elsevier, Springer, McGraw-Hill or the American Chemical Society, and partly because adoption of an SGML system does not yet offer a commercial return. Why invest in a 'neutral database' publishing system if it will not confer any apparent longer-term financial benefits? The attractions of producing different formats from the same single keyboarded operation are seen to be too intangible at present. This view is changing, particularly as the market for supplying 'header files' (author, title, affiliation and abstract of each article) to intermediary organizations begins to take off, and also as CD-ROM production from the SGML file becomes a commercially viable option.

In effect, the main traditional publishers are moving towards the 'electronic warehouse' concept. This is a computer store of text-tagged files which can be dipped into as and when new and enhanced publications are required. The 'electronic warehouse' is an updated version of the 'Knowledge Warehouse' idea, which was being examined in the mid-1980s, under the auspices of the Department of Trade and Industry (DTI) and the British Library, but failed at that stage because there was insufficient interest in such a cooperative archive.

Overall forecasts

According to the Fraunhofer Gesellschaft (Germany) some 95 per cent of all the world's STM information appears as print-on-paper. However, by 1996, the print proportion will fall to 86 per cent; 8 per cent will be optical; 2 per cent will be digital; 4 per cent will remain on microform.

Other forecasts are provided by the Consulting Trust GmbH (1993)in a study on publishing opportunities for the year 2000 (Figure 34).

Figure 34: European publishing market segments, 1992 and 2000

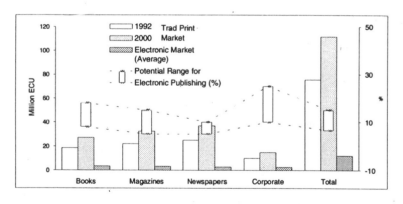

Source: Consulting Trust GmbH

Assuming a 5 per cent increase in traditional publishing per annum, the estimated potential for electronic publishing in the year 2000 is of the order of some £8 billion. The figures show that even under very conservative assumptions there are publishing opportunities which traditional publishers should not ignore.

Figure 35 illustrates the problem facing libraries in the next decade in the book market. There will be a migration (according to Consulting Trust (1993)) to electronic format of anywhere between 1 per cent (fiction) and 30 per cent (for STM) by the year 2000. The migration of STM books, to say nothing of the even more striking expected swing to EP within the journal sector, will make new demands on library managers.

Figure 35: *European book market segments, 1992 and 2000, and their potential for electronic publishing in the year 2000*

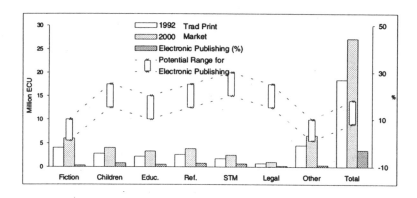

Source: Consulting Trust GmbH

Printed STM journal publications

The PA/ALPSP Survey on Journal Subscriptions

The Publishers Association (Serials Publishers Executive) and the Association of Learned and Professional Society Publishers jointly funded a study entitled *Trends in Journal Subscriptions*, covering 1992 data, published in January 1994 (Oakeshott, 1994). A questionnaire was mailed to members of both Associations and a 36 per cent response achieved (covering 809 journals). This showed that despite the library budget climate, the respondents were publishing 54 more titles in 1992 than in 1991 (a 7 per cent growth). There were 44 new titles launched and only 6 closures. The greatest area of new title launches was in medicine (one third of all launches). (See Figure 36.)

Figure 36: *Number of journals published by respondents, 1992*

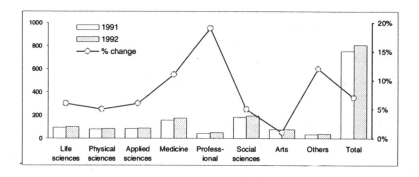

Source: *Trends in journal subscriptions,* PA/ALPSP, 1994

Seventeen of the 40 respondents were planning to expand their journal lists in future. This means that, despite the problems facing journal sales, the infrastructure and goal-setting within publishing are still such as to promote more, not fewer, publications at a time of excess of supply over demand.

Prices for journals rose 20 per cent over 1991. On a price-per-page basis the increase was 10 per cent. In some areas—such as the professional area—it was over 21 per cent on a per-page rate.

The average number of subscription sales per journal showed a 3 per cent decline over 1991. This compared with a 4 per cent decline recorded in the previous study organized by the PA/ALPSP, but this latter was over a two year period. More specifically, the rate of decline for full priced subscriptions was 5 per cent. Concessionary rate subscriptions bucked the trend, increasing by about 9 per cent over 1991. (This meant that they rose from 10 per cent to 11 per cent of the total number of subscribers, but due to their lower pricing they did not improve the overall revenue position.)

Figure 37: *Average number of full rate subscriptions*

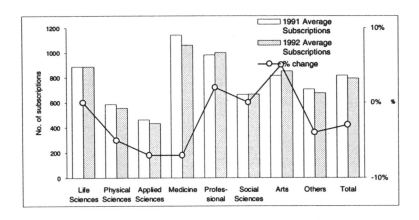

Source: *Trends in journal subscriptions*, PA/ALPSP, 1994

The traditional major export areas of USA and Canada, continental Europe, and Japan, all registered decreases of 1-3 per cent, and these were not offset by any increase in the UK.

Figure 38: *Geographical split of customers*

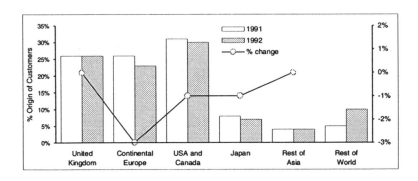

Source: *Trends in journal subscriptions*, PA/ALPSP, 1994

This shows how much print publishers depend on the industrialized world for their subscriptions. It is unlikely that the impoverished economies of the non-industrialized world will make much of an impact on overall subscription figures during the next few years, and there is therefore no support for the suggestion that the developing world will come to the rescue of journal publishers during the 1990s.

Revenues from other sources (advertising, backlist sales) were minimal in most instances, according to the PA/ALPSP survey. However, copyright payments through the Copyright Clearance Center (CCC) and Copyright Licensing Agency / Publishers Licensing Society (CLA/PLS) were for the first time noticeable, although the sums involved were still small. Article royalties are failing to balance the decline in subscription sales

Twelve of the 40 publishers responding to the survey had titles available in electronic form, online and/or CD-ROM. It is still impossible to gauge whether this has produced new income or is merely a displacement of the printed copy.

Ms Oakeshott's summary is that there seemed to be a continuing and steady decline in subscriptions in most subjects, accelerating in the case of established journals and those of general subject (rather than targeted specialist) appeal. The new income from selling private and personal subscriptions was minimal.

The Elsevier Subscription Trends

A similar picture emerges from an analysis of Elsevier journal sales, over a longer period. This shows that the main, or 'core', journal subscriptions on which Elsevier relies for 80 per cent of its profitability, are steadily falling in numbers (Figure 39). Even the launch of new journals is failing to compensate for this decline in the mature products, and overall the question is whether conventional journal publishers can manage to stay in business if they rely solely on conventionally-printed products.

The commercial problem facing publishers because of the eroding subscriber-base has been masked in the past by the continued increase in subscription prices, which have for some time been rising faster than the retail price index. A 10 per cent annual rise in per-page price has been the rule among the UK journals. Thus the price increases have more than compensated for the decline in unit sales, and explain the apparent health of the leading publishers' annual accounts.

Figure 39: *Trends in Elsevier journal subscriptions*

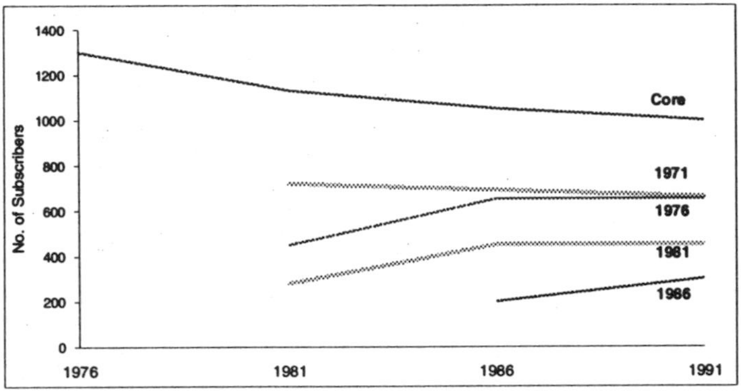

Source: Data delivered at Second European Serials Conference, 1992.

This is a slippery slope, and once the margin between sales and break-even becomes very small, the rate at which profitability falls will be spectacular.

Current market size

The number of journal and periodical titles currently being published is estimated at 126,000 (*Ulrich's International Periodical Directory*, Bowker). These include all subjects and Irregular as well as Regular titles.

The number of *new* titles launched is difficult to measure, but figures from ISI indicate a slowing down in the number of new journals. (It should be emphasized that this is not a statistically sound source as ISI specifically collect data from a relatively small collection of titles, and exclude the new (and more 'targeted') specialist titles from their coverage.)

The worldwide value of the research and academic journal business is estimated at £1,700 million (based on aggregation of subscription agency turnovers).

Key current players:

STM publishing is split between commercial publishers, learned societies, university presses, other institutes and 'peripheral' publishing.
The largest commercial publishers, with an estimate of their current
journal titles, are:

Elsevier Science	1,100 titles
Springer Verlag	350 titles
Blackwell Science	210 titles
Academic Press	210 titles
Wiley	250 titles
American Chemical Society	23 titles

These publishers are all involved to some extent in experimentation
with new media, though Elsevier in particular is firmly committed to the
printed journal subscription business, and is protecting it, and itself, as
much as copyright laws permit.

Learned societies experimenting with new media are more of a US
phenomenon. Some of the larger societies have publication programmes
which are similar in commercial intensity to those from the commercial
publishing sector in Europe. However, they are also at the forefront of
new experiments, with the American Mathematical Society and the
American Chemical Society leading the way.

The university presses are not notable publishers of STM serial
material though there is often a large book publishing programme centred
around the local academic institution. The fears expressed in the USA
that the commercial publishers are taking funds out of the science budget,
and putting them as profits into European shareholders' pockets, are
potentially revitalizing this sector.

Numerically, the small specialized publisher is the typical unit. This
publisher has limited recourse to funds for experiments, though there are
a few exceptions. Most are content to carry on with their printed publications, and are therefore potentially the most vulnerable in the New Age
of electronic publishing.

Market development issues:

Some of the key issues which relate to the future of printed journal
publishing are as follows:

- Printed journal subscriptions are increasingly dependent on institutional research library budgets. Research journals have to a large extent been priced out of the personal or individual market. Attempts over the past two decades to introduce 'personal subscription rates' at levels well below the library rate, have largely proved unsuccessful.

- Because of the difficulties with respect to library budgets, there is a general feeling that numbers of journal subscriptions are declining at 3-5 per cent per annum (see above). This means that publishers are caught in a 'price spiral'—declining sales pushing up subscription prices at a rate much higher than retail price indices.

- Publishers feel they can withstand the attack on printed journal subscriptions by continuing to increase price levels higher than the combined effect of reducing unit sales and general inflation.

- The commercial problem which STM publishers face is that there is clearly a limit to this strategy. Their journal profitability is vulnerable to swings of a few unit sales. As sales approach the commercial break-even level, the more vulnerable the publishers become.

- Most quality research journals, containing the high resolution graphics so often essential for leading edge STM, operate at break-evens of between 350 and 500 subscriptions. Very few new journals can aspire to these levels even after 3-4 years of promotion, and established journal subscriptions are falling from their earlier level of around 1,000 subscriptions to close to break-even. Once this level is breached, the journal becomes unviable and in financial terms should cease publication.

- If publishers can obtain new revenues from the same database of article literature—including from electronic publishing—this loss of viability can be forestalled. It is for this reason that many of the larger STM publishers are taking an active interest in SGML-formatted databases.

- Few 'names' in STM publishing are conducting significant electronic publishing experiments. Many are protecting themselves in printed journal publishing by assuming that copyright laws will support their operations.

• It is increasingly suggested (but not by publishers) that electronic copyright should be separated from printed copyright, and that the former should be vested with academic and funding institutions. This would enable new media to be developed despite the reluctance of the traditional print publishers.

The future for printed journals

As the Internet, the network 'superhighways', and high speed local area networks (LANs) and workstations become more pervasive, the ability of authors to communicate directly with end users without the need for a printed journal is growing.

This development is further fuelled by complaints from library directors in the USA that commercial journal publishers in Europe have engaged in considerable 'price gouging' in the past. The consequence is that the move towards DIY journal publishing within academia is becoming pronounced. It is estimated that 15 per cent of all university output goes through peer-reviewed journals, and the rest remains as 'grey literature'. According to ISI, 70 per cent of all published articles have an address which is from a university or related institution. It is clear that if the academics withdraw from publication in journals, most journals will disappear.

Several leading primary research publishers were contacted in the course of this study to determine how they saw the future development of journals. Given the decline in subscription sales and the ongoing pressure to communicate in a format acceptable to authors, how will the system develop? One of the leading publishers felt that their future would be intrinsically tied in with that of secondary publishers. As people search large subject-specific databases, they will identify articles of interest from relevant publishers and through a unique article identifier be able to order these direct from the primary publisher. In this case the publisher maintains contact with the market and is also able to dictate price-setting policies.

There is a growing fear that the network organizations (AT&T, Bell-CoRe, OCLC, Mercury, SURFnet) will become significant players in the information business, and that they will dominate and centralize the information process, to the detriment of publishers. The network operators will dictate the terms of trade and in so doing determine the commercial return (and editorial content) for the primary publishing business.

Printed scholarly book titles: academic and professional books

Spending on books

For books the position in the UK can be illustrated by reference to the *Book Trade Yearbook 1993*, from the Publishers Association, compiled by Dr Francis Fishwick (1993).

Books in general accounted for 0.49 per cent of personal consumer spending in 1992. This compares with 0.45 per cent in 1990 and 0.47 per cent in 1991. While the upward growth is favourable for book buying, not only does it still remain a small percentage of total leisure pursuits but it also covers a wide range of titles.

Figure 40: *Consumer expenditure on leisure pursuits (including books)*

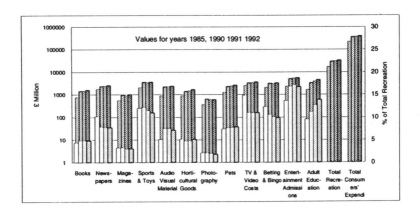

Source: CSO (Consumer Expenditure Estimates)

The breakdown of the book market in the UK, by source of funds, is shown in Table 9 (Fishwick, 1993).

Table 9: *Main market sectors (£ mil)*

Consumers' Expenditure	£1,600
Public Institutions (libraries etc)	£ 280
Estimates for:	
Private education	£ 30
Unrecorded students buy	£ 240
Business/professional	£ 220
Others	£ 160
Total Retail market	*£2,530*

The UK book market for academic and professional books—which represents 25 per cent of the total UK book market—rose from £367 million in 1985 to £556 million in 1990. Since then, despite recession within the UK economy, sales continued upward at current prices to £579 million and £631 million in 1991 and 1992 respectively. In real terms the percentage growth was -1.6 per cent in 1991 over 1990, and +5.1 per cent in 1992 over 1991.

Book buying by institutions (public, special and academic libraries) has seen a real decline in spending in the UK until 1990, after which the exceptionally high expenditure in the schools sector (coinciding with the National Curriculum changes) prompted a spurt in title acquisitions (mainly of school-related books). The 1991-92 spend by university and polytechnic institutions amounted to £26 million.

The overseas markets for UK books are reflected in Figure 41.

The number of titles has also increased over the years. According to Whitaker sources the following have been published (Figure 42).

Trends in unit sales

The next graph (Figure 43) complements those given earlier for journal subscriptions—both sets show that the number of sales of printed publications (books and journals) have been falling.

Figure 41: Export sales of all UK book titles, 1989 to 1992

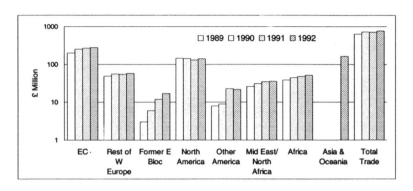

Figure 42: New book titles and new editions published in the UK

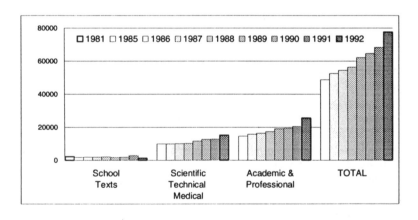

Source: Whitaker & Sons

As a result of the difficult market conditions being experienced by book publishers, both in the UK and overseas markets, book publishers reported a substantial drop in profits in the accounts ending in June 1991 compared with those for earlier periods. Profit margins on sales were less

Figure 43: *Development of book publishing: title production, copy volume, average print run*

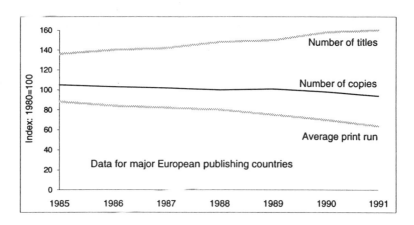

Source: BVDBH, SNE, CSO, Unesco, Consulting Trust GmbH.

than half those achieved in 1989-1990, and in contrast with the mid-1980s were far below those obtained by industry as a whole. As the *Booktrade Yearbook 1993* comments, although the total book market in the UK has increased in recent years, the cost of achieving this increase in sales has evidently been onerous (Fishwick, 1993).

Figure 44: *Financial performance of UK book publishers*

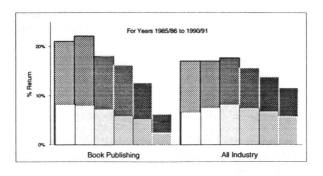

Current market size

Worldwide, there are 860,000 book titles published each year of all
varieties (Figure 45). It is estimated that 78,000 titles are published in
the UK per annum, and a comparable number in the USA. Over half the
new titles in the UK are academic, professional or STM.

The global value of STM books is believed to be £3,000 million (of
which Europe accounts for £1,200 mil). The annual growth is claimed
to be 2 per cent per annum.

Figure 45: *Number of book titles published*

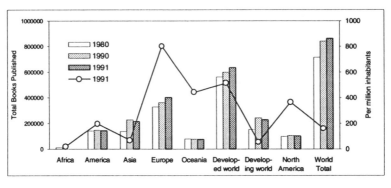

The 'richness' of Europe for editorial content, so frequently emphasized by Thomas Laukamm in his report on behalf of the EU on the future
information services market in Europe (1993), is illustrated in these
figures. Europe is responsible for nearly 50 per cent of the world's book
titles, the UK alone for 10 per cent.

Academic/professional and STM represent 53 per cent of the book
titles published (see Figure 42).

Key players

There is a wide spread of book publishing both in the UK and interna-
tionally. It is very much a 'cottage industry', with new entrants appearing
and disappearing with great regularity.

The USP ('unique selling point') of a publisher is his network of contacts and his commercial experience. These skills and knowledge base are fairly widely available. Some of the largest 'publishers' are the international corporations. IBM, Boeing, etc, have massive in-house publishing programmes (for manuals, for example), as do many software companies.

The barriers to entry into this business are low. However, the financial attractiveness of the business is also increasingly limited.

Market development issues

- Given that library budgets are also the source of much of the STM and academic book buying, the adverse international budgetary conditions which these libraries face means that book purchases are being keenly scrutinized.

- An earlier chart recorded the declining print runs and unit sales of books (Figure 43). What these figures obscure is the move out of book publishing by some of the traditional market leaders. Elsevier, in particular, with their high overheads, find it commercially unattractive to keep a book programme going and have discontinued several of their publishing lines from their Amsterdam base. There is a theory that publishers need to be small to be viable in STM book publishing—'small is beautiful'.

- The figures also hide the fact that reference publications are more robust than the single author research monograph. However, it is these reference works which are at the forefront of the electronic publishing challenge.

- This has meant that the book publishing industry has seen its profitability come under strain. Because of the tight economic climate, book publishers (unlike their journal publishing cousins) have tried to keep a control over price increases. This is in contrast to the actions in the captive market enjoyed by the journal publishers.

Document delivery

> *Gutenberg made everyone a reader, Xerox makes*
> *everyone a publisher.*
> *Marshall McLuhan, 'Washington Post', June 1977*

Current market size

Document delivery, and its cousin interlibrary loan, have been around ever since libraries realized that they could no longer remain 'libraries of record', and needed to share published information resources. The first loans from one library to another were done on an informal basis. Since then a veritable traffic of 'separates' has arisen as the new financial pressures have shown that the available funds are finite, unlike with published information. The arrival of new media—particularly online databases and CD-ROMs—has strengthened the need for libraries to borrow and lend their collections.

Document delivery by type of organization
All forms of individual article delivery from one centre to another comes under the umbrella term of 'separates'. This encompasses interlibrary lending, document delivery, electronic document delivery, reprint circulation and local photocopies made on campus of articles from published journals. The bedrock of 'separates' was interlibrary loan. With the arrival of the Xerox photocopier, document delivery then began to emerge. The distinction is that the former is a decentralized, largely uncoordinated activity whereas the latter is centralized, often under the control of a national library.

Commercial companies also entered the business, sometimes to enhance the search and retrieval services which they offered for abstracts, sometimes to fill the void left by the slower document delivery and even slower interlibrary loan services.

A recent development has been the emergence of integrated services which offer a listing of all newly published articles (CAS, standing for Current Awareness Service) combined with a simple process for rapidly delivering the full text of the required article within 48 hours of an online order being placed (IAS, for Individual Article Supply). CAS-IAS services became highly visible in the 1992-1994 period when many large intermediaries established systems to cope with the apparent new market for 'separates', for which they charged a high price.

New organizations are promoting this business, organizations which are not from the publishing sector, yet are making use of the published articles on which to build a new niche business. In recompense to the publishers for the original work the CAS-IAS suppliers do pay a royalty. The royalty level is set by the publisher but is usually at a rate which is related to the price expectation of a document within the market, and not to that which is required to achieve commercial viability for the publication process. In effect the publishers are setting royalties far too low for their internal business needs, but too high for the market which has become used to free or low-priced article supply.

Market size by document type
The extent of the document delivery business is large in physical terms. Table 10 shows the main categories.

Table 10: *Types of document delivery/interlibrary loan activity*

Interlibrary Loans	35.0	million
Formal Document Delivery	20.0	million
Online Database Vendors	0.25	million
Commercial Document Delivery	see under CAS-IAS	
CAS-IAS Services	4.0	million
Enhanced CAS-IAS Services	0.1	million
Primary Publishers Docdel	0.1	million
Customized Docdel	-	
Electronic Journals	0.1	million
Total 'separates'	60.00	million
On-campus photocopies	250.0	million?
Reprint Distribution (publishers)	25.0	million

Figures estimated as in 1992/3 by DJB Associates

Value of market
It is possible to make some basic assumptions about the true market size for document delivery, 'true' in this sense meaning the amount of revenue

which would be generated within document delivery if a realistic price were set for the processing of each document.

It can be claimed that the price of an interlibrary loan should be zero, as in practice no money changes hands when one library loans an item to another library. Interlibrary loans are notionally 'free'. However, there is a real cost involved in processing an order, both by the ordering library and by the library which fulfils the request. These costs are the 'overhead' of staff which are diverted to these processes, often from other essential library activities. Several recent studies have been undertaken within the US university library market (at University of Arizona; by the Association of Research Libraries) which put the total costs of meeting a loan request by both parties in this informal and unstructured arrangement at between $25 and $40. Libraries do not normally make such estimates of the real costs of interlibrary loans, which ensures the continued survival of the information industry myth of a 'free' interlibrary loan.

If one applied the sort of commercial charges which the new CAS-IAS services are forced to charge—approximately $12 on average—then this would give a financial estimate of the market. Multiplying the 60 million documents (excluding on campus photocopying and pre-print distribution) by $12 gives an annual figure of $720 million or about £430 million.

The journal subscription business itself, from which the articles are derived, has been estimated at $2,500 million (or £1,700 mil) worldwide. This means that royalties to the publisher imply a business sector for document delivery of 25 per cent of the journal business on which it relies.

Yet it is claimed that Elsevier only receive 0.2 per cent of their income from royalties, the reward for making the documents available through third parties. Other publishers have shown a range up to 2 per cent of their total revenues coming in the form of article royalties. But none approaches anything near the 25 per cent mark.

If the market assumptions described earlier are accurate, and the library market moves further towards the 'access' to information mode for collection development, then the document delivery sector will grow, possibly at the expense of the printed journal subscription market. Many publishers believe that document delivery is parasitic on the journal system, draining away its life blood. Emotive though this is, it does highlight a disturbing feature of the information business; namely, that there is no recognition that articles and journals are in a delicate balance, and shifts in direction could make the whole structure unstable. The fear of this happening in the later years of this decade haunts the publishers, and is a further reason to believe that new media will become a growing feature of the information scene.

Estimated growth rates

One can extrapolate the trends. Assuming a 10 per cent per annum growth in article business, fuelled by the many new professional organizations entering the business, then the article business will rise to £1,210 million by the year 2003.

The journal subscription business will see a 3 per cent per annum decline in physical subscriptions, though this will be counterbalanced by a 6 per cent real price increase. This results in a business of £2,060 million by 2000. Approximately half the journal business by then will be equivalent to the 'separates' business. This is highly unstable; the parasite becomes comparable in size with its host.

This has led to some pundits suggesting that there will be a rapid disintegration of the journal publishing process within the next five to ten years. Once the electronic options become more sustainable, once the infrastructure is in place, and once the main body of end users become used to using the electronic delivery systems, the fate of the printed journal is sealed.

Key current players

Table 11 lists the main players in each of the broad sectors of document provision.

There are no accurate figures available on the final category, though, paradoxically, this is the sector which pays royalties to publishers. So far the numbers involved are very small.

In the UK there is an 'iceberg' analogy to the above figures. At the top of the iceberg are the royalty-paid documents which are estimated at no more than 10,000 to 20,000 per annum. Below that are the documents being requested between the university libraries as part of an interlibrary lending system. These amount to about 80,000. These are delivered free, and no royalty is paid, as in the UK such libraries are able to operate within the 'library privilege' of the 1988 Copyright Law provisions.

One step below this are the articles requested directly from the BLDSC (British Library Document Supply Centre). These amount to 828,000 per annum (UK academia) and a processing charge is levied on their delivery of about £4.20 per item. Only in a few cases are royalties paid, when the requester volunteers that the item wanted no longer falls

***Table 11:** Main types of document fulfilment services*

Interlibrary Loan Services	Annual Estimates
OCLC Inc	2.4 million (out of 7 million ILL items)
National Library of Medicine	2.0 million
Medical School libraries	1.4 million
Association of Research Libs	3.0 million

Formal Document Delivery

BLDSC	2.4 million (out of 3.4 million ILL)
INIST (France)	0.8 million
TIB Hannover (Germany)	1.0 million
ZBM, Köln (Germany)	0.4 million
TU Delft (Holland)	0.3 million
CISTI, Ottawa (Canada)	0.5 million
JISCT, Japan	1.3 million

Commercial Document Delivery

ISI, Philadelphia	0.25 million
Engineering Inform	0.05 million
UMI	0.25 million

CAS-IAS and Enhanced CAS-IAS

UnCover (CARL & Blackwells)
Faxon Research Services
Ebsco Subscription
Swets and Zeitlinger
OCLC FirstSearch
PICA ILL
BLDSC's Inside Information
UMI ProQuest MultiAccess

within the 'library privilege' provisions. In this case £1.20 is paid to the Copyright Licensing Agency for onward disbursement to the copyright owner (usually the publisher). Below that there is a vast stratum of suppressed document delivery traffic. Because of the costs in obtaining items from the BLDSC, the interlibrary loans department often sets a 'cap' on the number of items requested in any one year. This may mean that the actual figures only reflect a small portion of the potential demand. There are at present nearly 35 million local loans taking place, and with an increasingly restrictive short term loan regime, the pressure on the document delivery business could become intense. Document delivery within UK academia seems to be an explosion about to happen.

The BLDSC has made a forecast of how it sees its document delivery business developing to the year 2003. This is shown in Table 12.

Table 12: BLDSC Strategic Development Path, 1992/3-2002/3

Year	UK	Overseas	Total
1992/93	2,632,000	819,000	3,451,000
1993/94	2,753,000	946,000	3,699,000
1994/95	2,872,000	1,092,000	3,964,000
1995/96	2,987,000	1,261,000	4,248,000
1996/97	3,097,000	1,456,000	4,553,000
1997/98	3,199,000	1,681,000	4,880,000
1998/99	3,289,000	1,941,000	5,230,000
1999/2000	3,364,000	2,241,000	5,605,000
2000/2001	3,420,000	2,587,000	6,007,000
2001/02	3,451,000	2,987,000	6,438,000
2002/03	3,452,000	3,448,000	6,900,000

UK demand will have to be increased by a further 30 per cent to achieve the above. Extrapolating the past trend to accommodate the above growth targets gives the following graph (Figure 46). The upper line represents the total requests which BLDSC must achieve (from a static level of requests in the early years), then the UK requests and the rapid growth reflects the anticipated expansion in overseas requests.

Figure 46: *BLDSC forecasted growth in its document delivery requests*

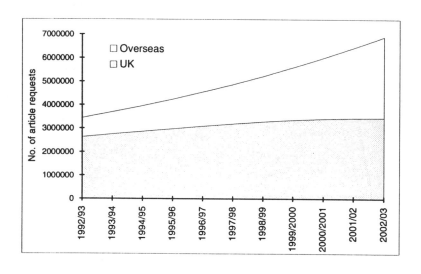

Can this expansion in activity be achieved? Some pundits have claimed that BLDSC is operating within a saturated UK market for document requests. Hence the static level of demand in the UK over recent years. On the other hand, on a per capita basis, the UK is still behind the Scandinavian countries (according to data presented by its then director, David Bradbury, at the First Document Delivery Conference in London in 1991). On this basis there is still room for growth as the suppressed 'capped' demand is released.

Structure of document delivery

It has been shown that 'document delivery' is not a straightforward process—it comes in many flavours. Some of these are documented below in Table 13.

Given this phased approach to the emergence of a variety of document delivery services, with the ultimate achievement being an electronic journal available only through the networks, the implication is that the document delivery business could be a transient business.

This has spawned the life cycle for document delivery which can be illustrated as follows (Figure 47).

***Figure 47:** Life cycle of electronic document delivery*

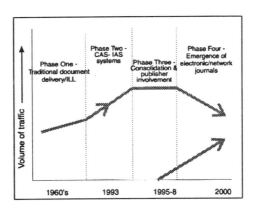

The decline of the document delivery business could be created from one of two forces:

- The very success of the document delivery (docdel) and interlibrary loan process could kill the journal because journal cancellations may be made, thereby drying up the source material.

- As technology improves so the ability arises to create fully electronic journals where there is no printed version on which docdel could be based.

Both these issues need to be taken into account, and for our forecast to the year 2003 we must assume that docdel will not have the visibility or relevance that it has today.

Table 13: The staged development of document delivery

First Stage—Interlibrary Loan
Main features: No Table of Contents service. Minimal Abstracting & Indexing. Dispersed collections. Free Article Supply. Low cost to user. Low efficiency. No royalties to publishers.

OCLC Inc., Dublin, Ohio
NLM Lonesome Doc (regional networks)
Library networks, particularly USA

Estimated Number of Articles per annum: 35 mil

Second Stage—Formal Document Delivery
Main features: No Table of Contents. No Abstracting & Indexing. Centralized collections. Low price article supply. Minimal cost to user. Improved efficiency. No or minimal royalties to publishers.

BLDSC, Boston Spa
INIST, Nancy
TUB, Hannover; ZBM, Köln
CISTI

Estimated Number of Articles per annum: 20.3 mil

Third Stage—Online Database Vendors
Main features: No Table of Contents. Sophisticated Abstracting & Indexing services. Some article supply. High article delivery prices. High cost to user. Limited usage. Little or no royalties to publishers.

Dialog DIALORDER

Estimated Number of articles per annum: 0.25 mil

Fourth Stage—Emergence of CAS-IAS services
Main features: Free Table of Contents. No Abstracting & Indexing services. Centralized or dispersed collections. High article supply prices. High cost to user. More efficient than in Second Stage. Some royalty to publishers.

Subscription Agents:	Faxon Research Services
	UnCover (B.H. Blackwell)
	Ebsco Current Citations/EbscoDOC
	Swets & Zeitlinger (SwetScan/SwetDoc)
Library Utilities:	OCLC FirstSearch
	RLG Citadel
	PICA
	BIDS
Secondary Services:	ISI, Current Contents Online and Genuine Article
	UMI, Article Clearinghouse and ProQuest
	Embase
	CAS DDS

Engineering Information, EiDDS and Article Express
with DIALOG
BIOSIS Document Express
Ask*IEEE (IEEE/IEE/Dynamic)

Estimated Number of articles par annum: 4.0 mil

Fifth Stage—Enhanced CAS-IAS services

Main features: Free Table of Contents. Free abstracts. Some indexing. Centralized and decentralized comprehensive collection. High article supply prices. Abstract and article royalty income to publishers. Improved efficiency.

UnCover
OCLC FastDoc

Estimated Number of articles per annum: 0.1 mil

Sixth Stage—Primary Journal Publishers

Main features: Free Table of Contents. Low cost abstracts availability. No Indexing. Decentralized Supply. High article prices. High cost to user. Questionable efficiency. High royalties to publishers.

ADONIS
OASIS
Institute of Physics Publishing

Estimated Number of articles per annum: 0.1 mil

NOTE: Publishers are in the document delivery business through the Preprints and Reprints business. Estimated number of articles in circulation is 25 million.
NOTE: Publishers are potentially in the business of announcing article availability on Internet fileservers: Springer Previews, Kluwers FTP, Elsevier, CUP, etc.

Seventh Stage—'Customized Docdel'

Main features: Free Table of Contents. High priced abstracts. Increased indexing. Lower article prices/wider distribution. Unknown commercial impact on publishers.

UnCover (in development)

Estimated Number of articles per annum: zero

Eighth Stage—Electronic Journals

Main features: Integrated online article provision through network services. Pricing based on variations around subscriptions and on-demand article printouts.

OCLC Online Journals
Red Sage
CAJUN
TULIP

Estimated Number of articles per annum: 0.1 million

Market development issues

- As document delivery grows so it impacts on the journal business on which it relies. One scenario is that the success of document delivery will result in the death of the journal, and therefore the death of document delivery as we know it.

- Journal publishers are taking a growing interest in the return which document delivery could bring to them. However, to date there has been no acceptable model which provides them with a suitable entrée.

- Despite the considerable 'hype' given to the CAS-IAS element of document delivery, there is no indication as yet that there is a dramatic growth in the business for article delivery. Price constraints may keep the document flow within the large (and difficult-to-quantify) interlibrary loan business.

- Document delivery may turn out to be an interim technology which will be outdated as and when electronic journal publishing becomes effective.

- In the short term there may be further growth in the amount of docdel, spurred on by:

  » fewer comprehensive research library collections and the emergence of a small number of 'superleague' libraries
  » growing emphasis on 'access' over 'holdings'
  » more CAS-IAS entrants (particularly from the primary publishing area)
  » the possible emergence of a small market of end users buying research material using their credit cards.

ELECTRONIC PUBLICATIONS

Future—That period of time in which our
affairs prosper, our friends are true and
our happiness is assured.
Ambrose Bierce, 'The Devil's Dictionary'.

Introduction

There is a school of thought which suggests that there will be a significant and rapid change in the way scholarly information is disseminated over the next few years, and that telecommunication and digital technology will be the key drivers in this. The advantages of the new information systems using such technology appear highly appealing. However, whilst this may be seen as a laudable feature of the informatics/telematics revolution, the consequences to the even growth of scholarly information dissemination could be disastrous. There is no guarantee that there will be a gradual and balanced migration from print to electronic in a way which satisfics the needs of all the agencies in the existing information chain; and the users of research information could be the ultimate sufferers.

An analogy has been proposed for this development. We are entering the 'valley of death'. The downside of the valley will be the decline in print subscriptions to research journals and books at a time before the infrastructure and changes in user behaviour are sufficiently in place. The upside of the valley will be the future date when there is a healthy business which supports an electronic information system in scholarly areas, and, the higher the climb from the valley floor, the more entrenched the electronic information systems become. The valley floor will see the destruction of some of the traditional (print-based) players in the information chain who have been unable or unwilling to adapt to the new electronic information environment.

Various pundits put different dates on the destruction of the print journal as we now know it. Andrew Odlyzko puts the life span of journals at between ten and twenty years, and argues that we should not shed tears for the demise of a print system which is essentially archaic (1995). He points to some of the virtues which will arise from the new electronic information systems, notably that the concept of the article as we now know it will change. The original article will pick up comments and enhancements as it proceeds along the air waves between collegial researchers, with these comments and additions providing an expanding view on the research effort as originally undertaken.

However, this is only one scenario, and electronic publishing offers a variety of forms. Some of these will be commented upon in the next sections and attempts will be made to quantify their existing encroachment into the scholarly publishing sector.

Bibliographic databases

Market size

In 1991 the EC-based hosts and information providers generated 3,325 MECU (£2,300 million) in revenues. Within Europe, 30 per cent of the bibliographic databases made available from countries within the European Commission originated in the UK; 18 per cent are created in Germany; 14 per cent in France; 11 per cent in Italy; and 10 per cent in Spain. The combined European online database market (including host database services as well as databases themselves) was about £6-10 billion in 1992. A steady growth of 20 per cent per annum has been achieved.

Figure 48 summarizes the market for online services in Europe for 1989-1990.

The clear domination of the UK as provider of online information services within Europe in 1989/90 is demonstrated above. However, to put the whole of the European scene in context with the USA, not only was the US online industry three times larger than Europe's but it was growing at 18.8 per cent, or 50 per cent more than Europe. The USA achieved a 57 per cent share of the global online database industry, whereas the combined resources of Europe was responsible for 27 per cent.

The forecast growth of the US Online Services Market is shown in Figure 49.

Online information services include the real-time financial and business services, which have been specifically excluded from this study. The bibliographic reference databases, also available through an online connection, are included, even though they represent only a small proportion of the industry, taking at most 20 per cent of the online business revenues.

Figure 48: *Market volume for European online information services, 1989-1990*

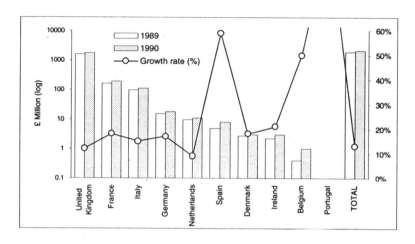

Source: European Information Industry Association

Figure 49: *USA online services market*

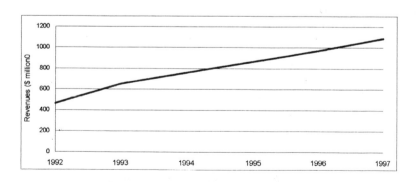

Source: Simba/Communication Trends

Unlike the situation with CD-ROMs (see later) the non-profit sector predominates in the online database business. The European countries are weak in the production of source (referral and full text) databases in comparison with the USA, a source of much concern to the European Commission during the past decade.

Number of bibliographic databases

There are over 8,000 publicly-accessible databases worldwide, of which over 5,000 are bibliographic (primarily text-based). One of the most authoritative sources for information on the worldwide developments of such bibliographic reference files is Professor Martha Williams (USA). Figure 50 shows the relative position as in 1991 between databases (individual files), the database producers or publishers, the computer host services which make the files available through a consolidated access routine, and the number of gateways allowing access through a different host service to a variety of different files.

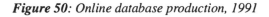

Figure 50: *Online database production, 1991*

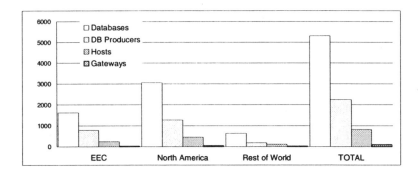

Professor Williams has also produced statistics on an annual basis to show the gradual but unspectacular emergence of bibliographic reference databases during the past twenty years (1993).

Figure 51: *Online database production (historical development)*

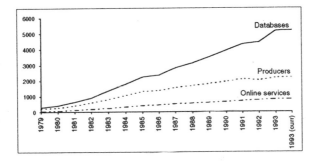

The number of UK databases is about 350 out of the worldwide count of nearly 8,000.

An alternative treatment of the database business is given in the *Gale Directory of Online Databases* (Figure 52).

Figure 52: *Worldwide availability of databases, producers and online hosts*

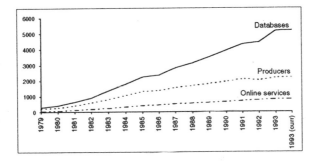

Source: Gale Directory of Databases, Vol 1: Online Databases (July 1993)

The number of records has increased by a factor of 87 (from 52 million to 4,527 million) while the number of databases themselves has grown by a factor of 26 (from 301 to 7,907). The average database in 1975 contained 173,000 records. This reached 500,000 in 1985 and 647,000 in 1992. There is therefore still growth to be witnessed in both the files and their respective sizes (Figure 53). The longer the file remains in existence and is updated the greater the number of records in the database.

Figure 53: *Growth in database records*

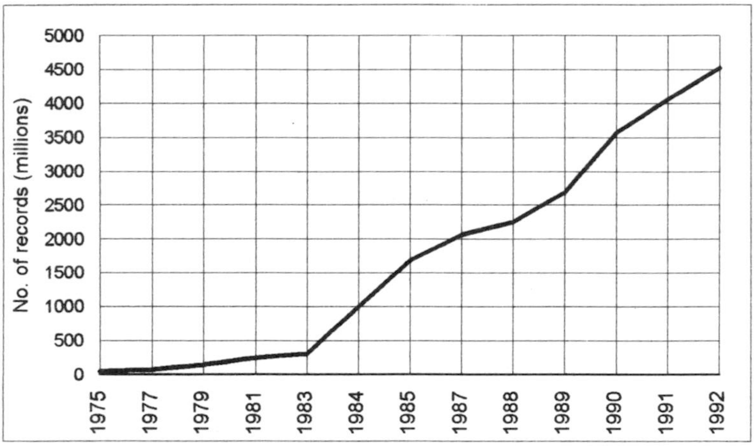

Source: Williams, 1993

Increase in database sizes was also due to an increase in commercially-available business databases that came on to the market in the mid-1980s. The introduction of time series databases (large) and telephone directories online in late 1980s continued the growth momentum.

Market usage of bibliographic databases

There is limited data available on the number of times bibliographic databases have been used over the years. The following figure (Figure 54) is from the audit compiled by Martha Williams (1993).

Figure 54: Number of online searches of USA vendors of word-based databases

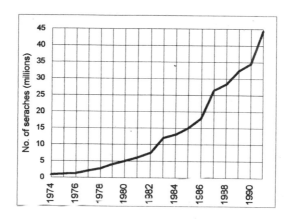

Source: Williams, 1993

New forms of databases

With the emergence of multimedia as a new information platform, there has been a change in the types of database content. A less constrained searching process is now possible, with text searching being complemented by other forms of media access. Figure 55 shows that image databases were just beginning to arrive in 1992, and audio datasets were also increasing. Word-based files, however, continue to dominate.

Taking the word-oriented databases a stage further, Figure 56 shows that there is a variety of types of such files and that full text, from being a small portion of the total in 1985, now dominates. Directory databases have also grown in number. The patent and trademark files have not increased in number (but the database sizes have grown larger).

Of the above databases, 33 per cent were in the business area, 19 per cent were in science and technology, 9 per cent were in health and life sciences and 11 per cent were law.

Figure 55: *Types of databases*

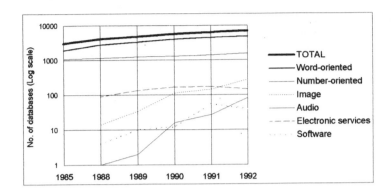

Source: Williams, 1993

Figure 56: *Breakdown of word databases*

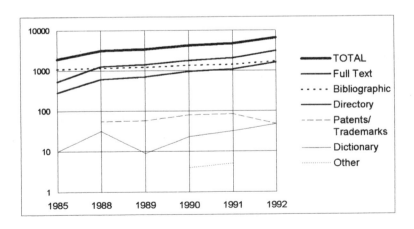

Source: Williams, 1993

Key players

Table 14 represents the main players in the bibliographic reference database publishing sectors. There is a great deal of volatility in their ownership patterns. The online hosting services have come under particular pressure in recent years with Dialog now dominating the sector, as others have been forced to merge with them or cease operations. Even within the database sector there is also some change, with Mead Data Central selling Lexis/Nexis to Reed Elsevier in 1994.

Table 14: *Leading international database vendors ranked by 1990 turnover*

Vendors	Turnover (MECU)	Country	Target
Mead Data Central	312.7	USA	USA/Eur/Japan
Dialog	102.9	USA	World
OR Telematiques	28.8	France	France
Radio Suisse (Datastar)	26.4	Switzerland	Eur/USA
WEFA Group	24.8	USA	OECD
Questel	22.6	France	Europe
Data Resources Inc	8.7	USA	USA/Eur
Européene de Données	8.0	France	France
GBI	3.2	Germany	Germany
ESA/IRS	1.6	Italy	Europe

Market development issues

- According to the European-based Information Market Observatory (IMO), sales of real-time (mainly financial) services in Europe grew by 4.5 per cent (to £1,076 mil) in 1991. Online retrospective or bibliographic services grew at a slower rate of 2.8 per cent (to £732 mil). (See Figure 57.)

Figure 57: *Total electronic information business in Europe*

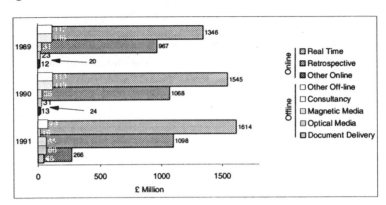

- Financial and business information services account for 91.3 per cent of all EC online and off-line revenues. (The UK, home to Telerate and Reuters, represents the major part of European real-time electronic information services.)

- STM information makes up a mere 3.3 per cent.

- In the UK, 25 bibliographic databases are believed to account for 80 per cent of all usage (East and Vogel, 1991). Forty-eight per cent of all online database access in the UK was through DIALOG.

- There is a high positive correlation between the size of databases and the proportion of their income which comes from online as opposed to the income from print products. Figure 58 shows the division of revenue in a study of 144 databases in 1990.

- Within the UK a national policy has been instituted to allow significant databases to be made available on all university campuses, through JANET and SuperJANET, as a nationally-negotiated licence. The Follett Review (1993) includes the recommendation for £1 million pa to be put aside to fund the establishment of further such subscription-based datasets among UK universities. A three year planning cycle is proposed.

Figure 58: Dispersion of revenues by database publisher size

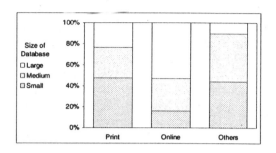

Source: East and Vogel, 1991

- UK universities have reduced their commitment to mediated online database searches. According to Harry East (1992) the average expenditure by universities fell from £9,300 in 1988 to £8,900 in 1990 (based on a sample of 10 sites).

OPTICAL PUBLICATIONS

> *The medium is the message. This is merely to say that the personal and social consequences of any medium.... result from the new scale that is introduced into our affairs by each extension of ourselves or by any new technology.*
> *Marshall McLuhan, 'Understanding Media'.*

Introduction

CD-ROM technology has taken the information industry by storm. Since standards were first agreed on the hardware in 1985, with subsequent agreements to standardize on operating systems to be installed on the discs, the build up of CD-ROM as a means of distributing vast amounts of textual information has been dramatic. A second wave of this interest in CD-ROM technology is being evidenced at present as multimedia—combining sound, moving images and animations, together with text and data on the same disc, to provide an integrated story—takes hold. Altogether some 8,000 CD-ROM titles were published in 1994.

We have come a long way in ten years, but can it last? Can CD-ROM last the course when its challenger, the wide area network, is flexing its technical muscles to take on the transmission of latest or real-time information? CD-ROM may be relegated to an archival storage medium.

This is speculative, and the timeframe for the transfer from print to CD-ROM to network distribution is imprecise. Nevertheless, by the year 2003 the competition between optical storage technology and network transmission technology will be evident, and already the battle may have been won.

CD-ROM

Market size

Total CD-ROM sales worldwide
The worldwide market for commercial (publicly-available) CD-ROM discs in 1992 was estimated at £670 mil. In addition, it was estimated by InfoTech, Vermont, that a further £1.5 bil was attributable to the in-house CD-ROM business worldwide. This gives a total CD-ROM industry revenue of about £2,200 million, which compares with a 1987 figure of £44 million.

In 1988 the estimate of the total industry was only £200 million, showing that business has grown tenfold in five years. (These estimates include figures for hardware and software and the 170,000 drives.) In-house publishing represents 23.4 per cent of the market and 44 per cent of the number of titles. Figure 59 shows how these figures have escalated in recent years. CD-ROM has been, and remains, a growth industry.

CD-ROM readers (drives)
Figure 60 shows the geographical dispersion of CD-ROM readers in the period 1990 and forecast to 1995. In 1992 the installed base of readers was 2.25 million globally.

Figure 59: *CD-ROM sales worldwide*

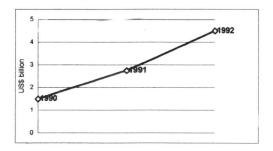

Source: InfoTech, 1992

Figure 60: *Penetration of CD-ROM drives*

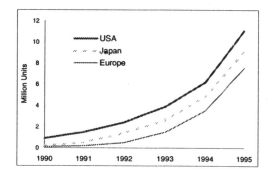

Source: Consulting Trust GmbH

A more recent forecast made by a different research group (Inteco, Adam Daum) puts the country-wide estimates in a more historical growth perspective (Figure 61).

In addition to the above CD-ROM readers used for accessing public databases, there were 2.7 million drives being used in-house within the corporate sector for more proprietary information services in 1992 (InfoTech).

Table 15: *Number of CD-ROM readers estimated*

	1991	1992
USA	1.44m	
Asia	0.72m	
Europe	0.20m	0.60m
UK		185,000
Germany		125,000
Italy		85,000
France		50,000
Netherlands		25,000

Source: InfoTech

In 1995 there were some 12 million CD-ROM drives in Europe. This can loosely be compared with an estimated 26 million personal computers worldwide, just showing how rapidly the CD has become a recognized PC peripheral. There is an increasing trend to buy new PCs with an inbuilt CD-ROM drive, which is a strong stimulus to the development of CD-ROM products for both the home entertainment and business/professional sectors.

Figure 61: *Worldwide CD-ROM drives—total by country*

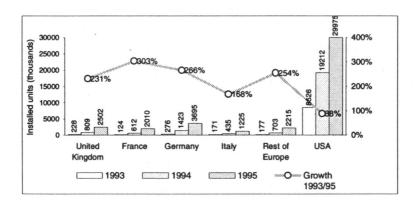

Projections into the future for CD-ROM are particularly treacherous territory as we do not know how long the life cycle is for this particular business within scholarly information. Nevertheless, courageous attempts have been made by Dataquest, Simba Information and Link Resources.

Figure 62: *Worldwide penetration of CD-ROM drives*

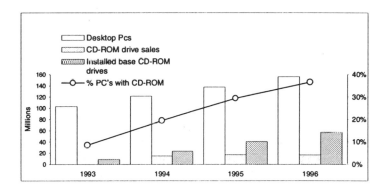

The UK CD-ROM drive market
As the earlier figures indicate, in the UK alone some 185,000 CD-ROM drives were in place according to an estimate for 1992/3 produced by InfoTech. Keynote—a separate forecasting company—only forecast 31,500 CD-ROM drives for the UK in 1992. Yet another assessment is given in Figure 63.

This illustrates the variability in forecasts in this sector of the information industry, made by the different forecasting companies.

Three-quarters of secondary schools in the UK now have the hardware to use CD-ROMs and the UK Government is to provide £4.5 million to encourage their use in primary schools. This follows an allocation of £8 million for CD-ROMs in secondary schools.

Figure 63: *UK installed base of CD-ROM drives*

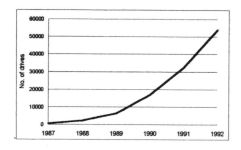

Source: Knowledge Research/Link

Number of CD-ROM titles
According to the latest issue of *The CD-ROM Directory* (TFPL, 1995), there were approximately 9,500 CD-based titles on the international market in the autumn of 1994. This represents only published titles currently available and does not include in-house publishing or discs which are out of print. This figure represents a 50 per cent growth over the previous year.

The geographical spread of the CD titles published in 1992 is shown in Figure 64.

Figure 64: *CD-ROM published titles (worldwide)*

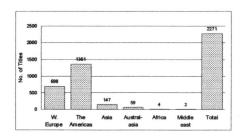

In the latest available TFPL directory on CD-ROM (for 1994) the geographical split was such that 50 per cent originated in the USA, 43 per cent in Europe, and 7 per cent in the rest of the world. The growth over the past few years is illustrated in Figure 65.

Figure 65: Growth of CD-ROM and multimedia titles, 1987- 1992

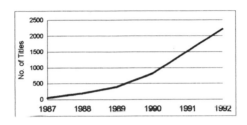

Projecting these titles to 1995 shows that in the final year there is an anticipated dramatic leap in the number of titles appearing on CD-ROM discs. This is largely a reflection of the fact that the 'chicken and egg' syndrome has been outgrown. A 63 per cent growth in CD-ROM titles was achieved between 1992 and 1993. Between 1993 and 1995 the growth is expected to be over 300 per cent. (See Figure 66.)

Figure 66: CD-ROM titles worldwide (including in-house), 1990- 1995

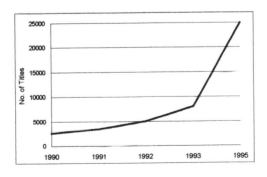

Source: InfoTech, Sony, Consulting Trust GmbH

UK CD-ROM titles
There are 400 UK-produced CD-ROMs from a total of 3,600 listed by TFPL in their 1993 Directory of CD-ROMs and Multimedia.

CD-ROM content
Most of the original CD-ROMs produced in the mid to late 1980s were bibliographic, with full text then taking a greater share. CD-ROMs containing images were the next most popular format. Over 40 per cent of the market is taken up by full text databases, and this has been the most rapidly expanding part of the CD-ROM sector. Bibliographic and reference account for 25 per cent and 16 per cent respectively (TFPL, 1993). These data are illustrated in Figures 67-69 and Table 16.

Figure 67: *CD-ROM titles by product category*

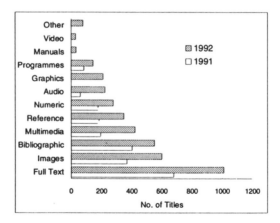

Totals add up to more than 152 and 2,212 respectively, due to some discs containing more than one type of information.

Figure 68: Content of CD-ROM (A)

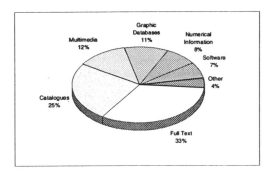

Source: InfoTech, 1992

In proportional terms, this breaks down into the following (Figure 69).

Figure 69: Content of CD-ROM (B)

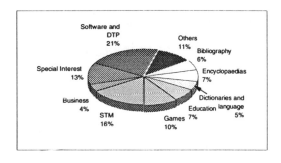

Source: Sample of 600 titles from the TFPL Directory on CD-ROMs.

Present production covers a fairly broad range of areas. The research interests are confined to approximately one quarter of the titles, with games and software being another major component.

A more detailed analysis of subjects is given in Table 16.

Table 16: Content of CD-ROMs

Product category	% of total
Bibliography	6%
Encyclopaedias	7%
Dictionaries and language	5%
Education	7%
Games	10%
STM	16%
Business	4%
Special Interest	13%
Software and DTP	21%
Others	11%

Source: Sample of 600 titles from the TFPL Directory on CD-ROMs.

Pricing of CD-ROMs

Prices of CD-ROMs are beginning to fall as the market size expands. Nevertheless, there are still some high priced CD-ROM titles available. (See Figure 70.)

Twenty-two per cent of CD-ROMs produced offered a price for licence to use the product in a network.

Market structure

- The European CD-ROM business in 1988 was as follows (Source: IMO Report 89/4):

  » 80 per cent of all CD-ROMs originated in the USA; 14 per cent were from the EEC; 8 per cent were from other regions.

Figure 70: *Price range of CD-ROM and multimedia CD titles, 1991-1992*

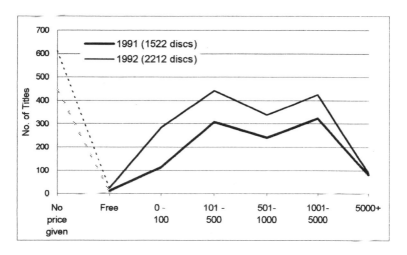

The term 'No price given' covers various options: the pricing structure may be so complicated that it is easier for the publisher to invite applications rather than to try to list all the different prices; the price may not be determined at the time of compilation of the directory; the disc or discs may be intended for internal use or limited distribution where price is not a factor.

» 170,000 CD-ROM drives were installed worldwide and 580 titles were published in 1988 (270 of which were for in-house applications).
» Germany, Italy and the UK led Europe in title publication.
» The EEC concentrated on source (referral databases) and full text (74 per cent) CD-ROMs, whereas in the USA the emphasis was on bibliographic (35 per cent).
» In both the US and EEC, the for-profit sector is responsible for 75 per cent of all CD-ROM titles.

• A continued growth in academic and library markets is anticipated. However, there are more companies interested in information content on CD-ROM in Europe than in USA or Japan (733, 607 and 87 respectively).

- In January 1992 there were 1.1 million CD-ROM discs pressed— by December the figure was 4.4 million.

- Current estimates suggest that there are 450-500,000 IBM compatible CD-ROM drives installed worldwide and the number is growing at 15,000 to 20,000 per month.

- Interest in the CD-ROM product development is increasingly driven by games and leisure interests. There are indications from the USA that this interest is escalating. During the last three months of 1993 more CD-ROMs were sold than in the previous three-quarters combined. There is also a flurry of acquisitions of CD-ROM producing companies, such as Longmans and Paramount both buying large CD-ROM companies in the spring of 1994.

- Within the UK there are similar signs of activity. CD-ROM drive sales rose from 51,000 in 1992 to 140,000 in 1993, and is projected to top 200,000 in 1994 (and 320,000 in 1995).

- In the USA, 45 per cent of all PCs being shipped by the OEMs (original equipment manufacturers) will have CD-ROM drives installed. The UK rate is probably not much different.

- The reason for the emergence of CD-ROM drive purchase is partly that the quality of the graphics from CD-ROM is much better than from a floppy disc or hard disc system, allowing more lifelike graphics in computer games.

- On the Mac front there are 1.5 million CD-ROM drives: 68 per cent are in the USA, 11 per cent in Japan and Europe has 18 per cent. Half the latter is equally shared between Germany and the UK. There are 67,500 Mac CD-ROM drive owners in the UK. Seventy per cent of new Macs now have in-built CD-ROM drives.

- These figures emphasize the fact that CD-ROM publishing is here. The medium has become popular for publishing large amounts of text and data, and increasingly to accommodate multimedia information. By the year 2000 the CD-ROM business, despite all its technical faults, is likely to remain a key element in the information business.

Multimedia

Definition

Multimedia workstations are essentially defined as those offering the capability to display and reproduce some or all the following on a single medium:

- text
- data
- audio
- graphics
- still pictures
- animation
- moving pictures

Each has a set of technical standards which are increasingly becoming open. Though 'multimedia' is usually described as a feature of the latest CD (compact disc) products, multimedia also has its say in the network and other electronic delivery systems. At present restrictions on bandwidth and end user hardware capabilities are a limitation on multimedia in the networking area, though this is changing rapidly.

Market size: number of CD-based workstations

Global market
It is estimated by Simba Information (Wilton, CT) that by the end of 1993 there were 5.4 million multimedia players which were attached to PCs. The expectation of this consultancy group was that this would grow to 17.1 million by the end of 1995 (see Figure 71). The addition of appropriate cards in established PCs, and the supply of factory delivered PCs with enhanced multimedia capability built in, would both account for this dramatic increase.

In addition, the availability of 1.4 million platforms which offered multimedia capability from Philips (CD-I) and Sony and Nintendo (3DO) will increase the market base for multimedia products, and this particular figure is expected to increase to 5 million by the end of 1995 (Figure 72).

Figure 71: *Installed base of multimedia capable devices*

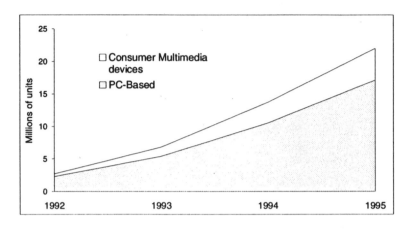

Source: Simba Information

Figure 72: *Worldwide installed base of consumer multimedia devices*

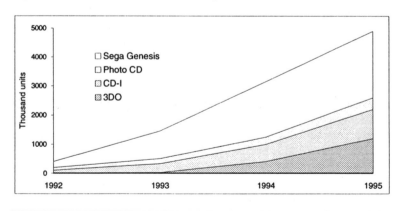

This is an industry where the consumer application of the technology is still trailing behind the professional use. By the year 1995 there may only be as many consumer multimedia devices as there were in the professional and scholarly world in 1993.

US Market

Simba also estimated just under 6,500,000 multimedia-capable machines installed in the USA in 1993, an increase over the previous year of 170 per cent.

Simba estimated that IBM-compatible machines dominated the new purchases of multimedia hardware, with 11 million units installed by the end of 1995. This compares to the estimated 5.5 million Mac units.

Figure 73*: Estimated multimedia-device installed base*

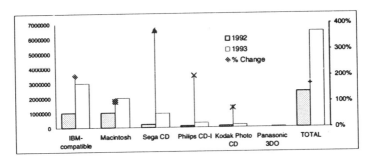

Source: Multimedia Business Report, Simba Communication Trends, Wilton, CT.

By comparison, the US-based Optical Publishing Association (OPA) had itself forecast that by the end of 1993 there would be 3.4 million PCs with CD-ROM drives (2.3 million Windows PC and 1.1 million Apple Macs). This is much less than the Simba estimate.

Fastest growing in 1993 was the Sega CD, with an estimated 950,000 players sold. This shows that the main initial focus for the CD-I activity will be in satisfying the need for computer-based games at home.

The Philips CD-I player, despite a 200 per cent jump in sales in the year, had still only sold 300,000 players by the end of 1993.

European market

The European market total for multimedia hardware and software in 1996 is estimated by Frost and Sullivan to be £1,600 mil. Their feeling is that training is likely to be the largest sector (23 per cent) for IMM (interactive multimedia) market penetration at that point, outperforming the games sector.

By the end of 1992 100,000 CD-I players had been sold in Europe. According to other estimates there are 73,000 CD-I machines (and 34,000 Sony Data Discman).

Market size: number of multimedia titles

The number of multimedia titles grew from 40 (in 1990) to 809 (in 1993). The feeling is that this will rise to 20 per cent of all CD-ROM titles in the next few years.

Figure 74: *Multimedia titles growth*

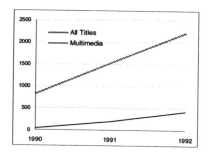

Market structure

Multimedia products will have a turnover of $27 million in the US and Europe in 1992. By 1997 sales will have increased to $6,824 million (Andrew Welham, Penguin, referring to a study undertaken by Ovum).

Networked multimedia sales are predicted to grow from $500 million in 1991 to $9,000 million in 1997 (USA and Europe).

Market developments

The strengths and weaknesses of Europe, the USA and Japan in the various technologies required for successful multimedia production are shown below:

- Computing   (Europe weak, USA strong)
- Consumer electronics   (Europe weak, Japan strong)
- Telecommunications   (USA strong)
- TV, film, music   (Japan weak)
- Publishing information   (Europe strong, Japan weak)
- Image companies
- Services

The above 'convergence' of technologies and systems explains why there is a new breed of electronic information providers of IMM. Traditional publishers have difficulty coping with the 'culture' of the new business.

CD-I (Compact Disc-Interactive)

Market size
CD-I is a newer initiative being promoted as a 'make-or-break' for Philips. It was pioneered by Philips with some support from Sony and Matsushita. It involves the CD being played through an attachment to the television (rather than as a computer peripheral as with CD-ROM), and is therefore primarily aimed at the home market. However, Philips has spread its risks more recently by offering a PC add-in card to make it both a domestic and business device. CD-I employs proprietary systems to allow the integration of data, text, audio, and still and moving images. It offers various levels of audio quality.

CD-I was launched in the USA in October 1991 and in the UK the following spring. Games and leisure subjects figure prominently in the early title development (many co-funded by Philips), though there are some titles with academic and professional interest. However, 40-50 per cent of the 300 or so titles available at the end of 1994 will have digital video capability.

In 1993 two other Japanese giants in the software entertainment business threatened a spoiling tactic with the launch of their 3DO. These were developed by Sega and Nintendo and challenge CD-I in the delivery of VHS (Video Home System) quality images through the screen for interactive entertainment.

Despite the many years of gestation, it still represents only a small portion of the CD industry, as shown by the following graph which suggests that in 1992 only 2.22 per cent of new CD titles were CD-Interactive (Figure 75).

Figure 75: New CD-ROM and multimedia CD titles, 1992

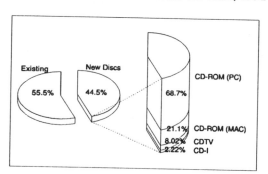

Nevertheless, Philips hoped to have 1 million CD-I players sold worldwide by the end of 1994 and that after a slow start it would become part of the home entertainment hardware infrastructure.

CD-I is a product/service which is for the future rather than the present. It is hoped that it will become a key aspect of in-home entertainment, but there is no guarantee that this will occur. In the meantime, the forecasters have been putting a value on the CD-I industry for the year 2000 of £30 billion (of which discs themselves will account for £6 billion). Such forecasts, given the new and emerging technologies and platforms competing for a share of the home entertainment market, must be questionable.

The breakdown of the component parts of the CD-Interactive business has been assessed as shown in Figure 76.

Geographically, the totals for players and discs separately can be broken down into the main areas shown in Figure 77.

Market development issues

- The CD-I business is seen as a peripheral market sector to the mainstream general public leisure and entertainment business.

- The costs of CD-I development are much greater than CD-ROM because of the multimedia nature of the product (see next section). Integrating moving images, high quality graphics and sound with text is technically more difficult than dealing with

Figure 76: Market for CD-I products

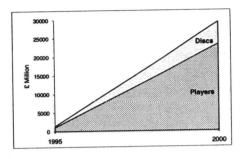

Source: Tony Feldman, BL, Philips

Figure 77: Geographical analysis of future CD-I markets

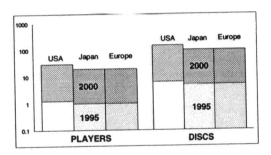

text/graphics alone, and, more significantly, it demands a different sort of 'production' skill. CD-I development is being led by the ex-movie and TV companies rather than by the classic print publishers.

- The number of professional/academic and research titles which will appear on CD-I by the year 2000 is assumed to be no more than 20 per cent of that year's production.

- This gives an estimated disc publication of 700 titles in 2000 and an industry value of £1.25 bil worldwide.

BROADCAST TECHNOLOGIES

Videotex services

Market size

- There were an estimated 2.9 million videotex customers in Europe in 1991, and 3.8 million users in 1992 (Source: Consulting Trust GmbH), a 30 per cent annual growth.

- France (Teletel/Minitel) is the dominant market for videotex services worldwide as a result of their national decision to distribute Minitel terminals instead of printing telephone directories in the early 1980s. Minitel now attracts 900 million connections pa (1991).

- Ninety per cent of all videotex users are in France. However, the most intensive usage of videotex terminals is found in Germany (455 minutes per terminal) and Italy (285), with France at 100.

- In the USA, the largest operators are Compuserve (760,000 customers), Prodigy (550,000) and Genie (252,000) (Source: Arlen Communications 1991).

Market structures

- Main market sectors for videotex are travel, financial services, commercial organizations (banks, insurance companies) and consumer information. It is therefore not a mainstream service for academic, professional or research publication.

- The profitability of Teletel in France (allowing for the investment in the infrastructure) is still unclear. Other countries are faced with a lack of consumer interest. (Anecdotally, the main usage of

Minitel in the development phase and later has been as a dating service.)

- Because of a lack of consistent international videotex standards, this service is predominantly nationally-based. The European Commission is attempting to address this.

Audiotex services

Market size

- The worldwide market is estimated at 2,810 MECU (VSB, Triniton Telecom).

- Japan's share is 989 MECU; the USA's is 754 MECU; the EU's is 765 MECU; and the rest of the world's is 302 MECU.

- Europe will rise from 550 MECU in 1990 (Consulting Trust GmbH), to 765 MECU in 1992, to 1,200 MECU in 1993 (CIT Research), to 2,000 MECU in 1995.

- The various national markets in Europe in 1992 are estimated to be as follows:

UK	347 MECU
France	279 MECU
Netherlands	100 MECU

Market developments

- Audiotex services are mainly aimed at national consumer markets. However, they are expected to move into professional information services in future (finance, travel, sports and telemarketing).

- Growth rates of 25-30 per cent per annum are anticipated.

- Interactive audiotex services are likely to increase in importance.

TELECOMMUNICATIONS-BASED SERVICES

Network publishing

....do not worry about it; do not disregard it.
Anon

Introduction

Networks, as a part of the scholarly information process, cannot be ignored. In fact they are increasingly becoming interlinked with some of the quantitative sciences, in particular, as a means of providing instantaneous access to a wide range of information and information sources. So rapidly has the global network—the Internet—caught on that it is threatening to tear itself asunder under the weight of usage (although not all is for scholarly communications).

The limitation is the power or speed of the networks. Communication networks are improving rapidly in this direction. Most research departments in the USA have their computers attached to Ethernet local area networks (LANs), which operate at almost 10 Mbs (million of bits per second). Furthermore, almost all universities now have access to the Internet, which was not the case just a few years ago. The Internet backbone operates at 45 Mbs, and prototypes of much faster systems are already in operation. The 'killer application' to create more bandwidth which will extend down to the individual house will be 'movies on demand'. Scientists might not like to depend on systems that owe their existence to trivial films being transmitted at hundreds of megabits per second, but if the technical infrastructure is in place, then they will use it to transfer large files.

At present the Internet is financed mainly from a $20 million subsidy from the National Science Foundation (NSF), though this is about to change and industrial organizations will provide the finances in future. Future size and traffic on the networks will drive the cost down even further from the present £1 per user per annum. This will in turn, as with the M25 motorway, spawn even more traffic.

Market statistics

- 'Internet' is the umbrella within which thousands of networks are connected using the TCP/IP (Transmission Control Protocol/Internet Protocol) protocols which enables users in different countries, using different networks, to exchange information. It is the most rapidly growing feature of the information firmament.

The Internet was launched in 1988 although its origins date back to the late 1960s.

• The Internet had between 1.3 million and 1.77 million connected computers in 1993. Currently 1,000 PCs are being connected to the Internet each week. Estimates of the number of individuals using the Internet vary from 15 to 32 million worldwide. In the 1992 IMO *Annual Report* the number was put at 8 million.

• The number of networks connected to the Internet grew from 3,500 in October 1991 to nearly 7,000 in September 1992. By November 1992 there were 8,561 networks supporting 727,000 host computers in 44 countries. There are now 60 countries on the 'Net'. A new network is being connected every few minutes (Figure 78).

• Whereas 17 per cent of homes have a personal computer, only 1 per cent have a modem (1989). This is changing, and modems are not only being bought as standalone devices but also increasingly being loaded into delivered new PCs as standard.

Figure 78: *Internet growth: number of networks included on the Internet*

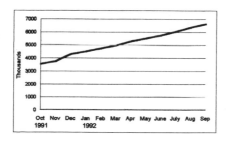

Source: Merit Network Inc.

- Over one million e-mail messages are sent over the Internet every month. It is also estimated that 80,000 'network articles' are written to the Internet each day.

Market structures

Figure 79 shows the type and number of products/services available over the Internet.

Several types of services are available through having an Internet connection.

- E-Mail (electronic mail)   18 per cent

- ftp (file transfer protocol)   47 per cent
  Three million files representing 165 Gbytes were available from 1,044 ftp sites. The 20 largest ftp archives account for 57 per cent of available files and 38 per cent of storage. Text files account for 10 per cent of files and 8 per cent of storage.

- Remote login or Telnet (bulletin boards, etc)   8 per cent

- Other   29 per cent

Figure 79: Overview of Internet resources (summer 1992)

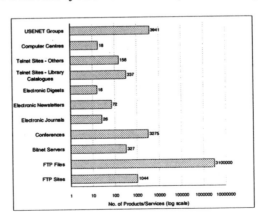

The proportions between these services can be seen in the pie charts in Figure 80.

Figure 80: Percentage of network traffic in packets and bytes by protocol

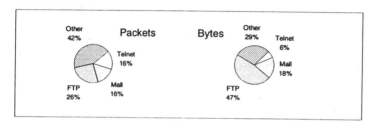

Source: Merit Network Inc.

Market usage data

The increase in traffic on the Internet between 1992 and 1993 was 997 per cent. A 15 per cent per month increase in use has been claimed. The uncoordinated nature of the Internet is such that meaningful comparative statistics are difficult to obtain. An estimate of the amount of network traffic in bytes is shown in Figure 81.

Figure 81: Growth in network traffic

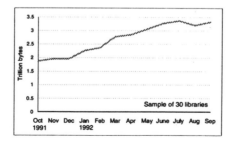

Source: OCLC

Related information services

Preprints

Preprint dissemination has already become the main method in physics and mathematics, and several other fields, for experts to communicate their latest results amongst themselves. Two approaches are becoming common. One is for departments to set up publicly accessible directories from which anyone can copy the latest preprints via anonymous ftp (file transfer protocol). The other is to use special preprint servers with scholars sending their preprints to a central database.

The issue which arises from the rapid adoption in certain areas of the electronic print exchange (e-print) culture is that it is destructive to the printed journal concept. The latter offers few advantages, compared with a well-managed and well-moderated electronic preprint exchange system.

The mould was broken when the first physics preprint service was established by Paul Ginsparg in his office at Los Alamos. Within a year it had become an unofficial industry standard, and seven other similar preprint services, each catering for a specific niche within the physics area, appeared in rapid succession. By February 1993 there were 8,000 subscribers in a dozen centres with 600 preprints submitted each month.

The speed and complexity of this business has meant that Paul Ginsparg has had to seek external funding to keep the popular service going.

Bulletin boards

Scholars could run the above preprint services themselves, without any extra funding required, by making use of the spare capacity on their existing machines. There is no more work for the author in this scenario than there is under the printed system. The publishers therefore feel threatened.

A number of more structured, publisher-organized information services have therefore galvanized into action during recent months in response to the challenge thrown down by the informal preprint systems. Examples of these are as follows:

- Elsevier has followed suit with a bulletin board service in the Nuclear Physics area, in order to protect a key editorial resource (the relevant printed journal).

- Current Science Ltd has organized a bulletin board service which came live at the end of May 1994 for researchers in the area of Structural Biology (BioMedNet).

- Bioscience is a small company which has offered a bulletin board service to the international biological community in the biodiversity area for the past six months (Bioline).

These various bulletin board initiatives are attempts to get the research community to concentrate their informal communications—letters, advance research results, notes of meetings, forthcoming conferences, etc—as well as their formal communications (research articles) around the board. Though access is free, various paid services can be made available through special passwords, granted on payment of the required subscription.

Market developments

- Electronic information services, such as bulletin boards, electronic mail, and electronic conferencing, contain data that are transitory or non-archival. They are communication items. Publishing deals with information. As the two become more and more interlinked, through the speed and convenience of electronic services, the growth in archival network publishing will become significant.

- Searching using the various 'navigators' is one of the fastest growing parts of the business. Examples of 'navigators' include:
    Gophers
    Archie
    World Wide Web (WWW)
    Wide Area Information Service (WAIS)
    Veronica
    X-Mosaic
    Hytelnet

- Commercial applications on the Internet are growing faster than educational ones, a reflection of the change in ownership of constituent networks linked to the Internet in the USA. The breakdown of usage as provided by OCLC is as follows:

    Research   45 per cent
    Commercial   28 per cent

Defence	10 per cent
Education	6 per cent
Government	7 per cent

- Not all the information or publications available on the Internet are of very high quality. In fact, the biggest complaint about the 'Net' is the amount of rubbish or 'noise' which one has to wade through on the system before getting anything of value. The old computer adage, 'garbage in, garbage out', still holds true.

This argues for a quality control role such as is offered by the publishing industry. In the meantime, the following charts, produced by a Belgian Research group, shows that only about one third of the material on the networks is considered 'useful' and that only half of this is printed off or passed on electronically (Figures 82 and 83).

Figure 82: Use of network; documents retrieved via network

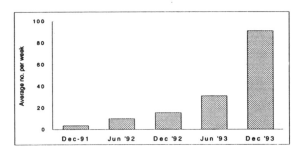

Electronic journals

There is massive support given by many organizations and end users to the existing print-based information system. Given this social investment in the libraries, for example, and the business investment in the publishing community, it seems unlikely that major changes will be visible in scholarly publishing within the next five years. Most papers will continue to be published in the traditional way. However, subscriptions to these print products will continue to drop, prices will continue to increase, and

Figure 83: Use of networks: time

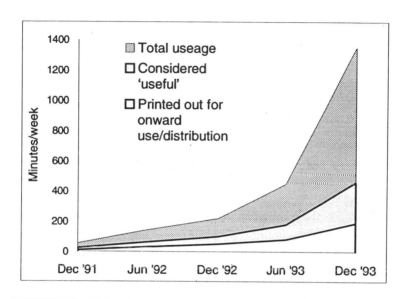

the system will be showing more and more signs of stress. At the same time electronic publications will be developing rapidly—though not necessarily sufficient to fill the void—and eventually they will become dominant. One industry watcher (Odlyzko, 1995) feels that this electronic dominance will be achieved between the years 2000 and 2010.

Market size

Figure 84 represents a summary of the 'publishing' activity on the networks as of 1993.

It is estimated that there were between 12,000 and 15,000 electronic discussion groups, conferences and bulletin boards, though this figure is very speculative.

Market developments

• According to Professor Jack Meadows (1995) it will be the social

Figure 84: *Electronic journals, newsletters and discussion groups on the networks, 1993*

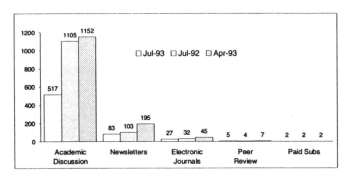

Source: ARL Directory

science and humanities areas which will migrate most rapidly to network publishing, because they have minimal requirements for graphics and illustrations (which take up considerable bandwidth).

- Other subject areas will develop as the technological infrastructure permits and as the researchers in each area accept the electronic journal as equivalent in status to the printed journal. So far the main subject areas with peer-reviewed electronic journals are:

Psychology	2 titles
Clinical medicine	1 title
Mathematics	1 title
Computer Science	1 title
Physics	1 title
Engineering (elec)	1 title
Engineering (mech)	1 title

- The Royal Society STM meeting showed the need for a model to study the economics of electronic journals. So far as is known, there are as yet no such economic models in existence.

- There are two types of electronic journal:

» 'parallel published' journals, with both printed and electronic versions available to the public;

» 'electronic' journals only, where there is an electronic version, the print option being available on demand.

An example of the latter is the *Journal of Online Current Clinical Trials (JOCCT)*. It has suffered from its online-only feature, because researchers have been reluctant to submit material to it if it does not confer the same reputation and prestige as publication of a printed article. It is interesting that while *JOCCT* is being sold by its owner (the American Association for the Advancement of Science (AAAS)), other new electronic journals are coming on stream using the same procedures and system but derived from a print publication—they are 'dual publications'.

• Examples of 'dual published' electronic journals are as follows:

» Three projects which make use of the Bell Labs program 'RightPages':

› *Red Sage* (with Springer and the University of California at San Francisco)
   - with a 'general' biomedical journal (*New England Journal of Medicine, British Medical Journal*, etc.)
   - with a molecular biology/radiology accent (the original *Red Sage*)
   - a broader-based electronic journal in the biomedical societies with a growing number of international publishers participating.

› AT&T's 'in-house' service. This has included technical journals circulated within AT&T's labs, with consent for electrostorage being acquired from the original publishers.

› A new 'commercial service' run by AT&T in the biosciences.

» ISI is also launching a new biomedical service, similar to AT&T's, again relying on publisher agreement. The network which ISI will use is being provided through an agreement with IBM.

» CAJUN is a joint developmental project involving several Chapman and Hall journals and a Wiley journal to use the

Adobe ACROBAT pdf (portable document format) to transmit exact replicas of source documents to end-user workstations, irrespective of type.

» TULIP (The University LIcensing Program). Elsevier is experimenting with 43 materials science journals from Elsevier and Pergamon which are being downloaded to nine university campuses in the USA via the Internet. An image file, ASCII file and a header file (CAPCAS) will be included for each article.

» ELVYN. The Institute of Physics Publishing has a research grant shared with Loughborough University to test the acceptance in five university library centres of a dual published (and new) journal on Modelling and Simulation in Material Science and Engineering (Rowland *et al.*, 1995). (ELVYN stands for 'ELectronic Versions Y Not?')

» OCLC is offering an *OCLC Online Journals* service whereby publishers can deliver their SGML formatted files of journals through the OCLC network, using GUIDON (OCLC proprietary) software.

• There are fewer examples of STM 'electronic journals' only. However, it is felt that more will emerge as the networks take a greater hold over the information system, and the 'moderated' bulletin boards become more formal and structured.

OTHER TECHNOLOGIES

Fax-based publishing

Market size

There were an estimated 26 million fax machines in use in 1992, a fivefold increase over the 5 million estimated in 1990 (of which 1 million were in Europe). The uptake of fax machines was one of the great information industry successes of the 1980s. In early 1980 the scope for delivery of an image version of a copied article was only just becoming apparent.

Market structure

Fax has been used to a limited extent within the publishing business as a way of improving the speed of manuscript flow from authors to editors to referees to the publisher. The fact that the fax copy retains the structure, layout and typography of the original version is a great advantage in the publication process. Companies such as Rapid Communications of Oxford (RCO) have adopted fax transmission as a feature of their publications process.

Fax (and audiotex) interactive publishing was worth an estimated £60 million in 1992 worldwide.

Fax transmission in the scholarly process is likely to show new growth in servicing individual article requests as libraries are forced to cancel more journal subscriptions and take advantage of the speed of fax delivery as an alternative way of getting required articles.

Fax technology

Fax (Group 3, which involves transmitting one A4 page of text/graphics within one minute of transmission time) is the standard currently adopted by most offices and research sites. Its limitation is that it does not provide a sufficiently high quality copy of the original, as the resolution standard in use is not very high.

This can be overcome by moving to Group 4 fax, which is a faster system (transmission time measured in seconds) and involves higher resolution. However, broadband telecommunications systems, which will form part of expanded networks, would be required. The cost of Group 4 machines is much greater than that of Group 3 (the latter being in the £200 to £500 range).

Fax and electronic publishing

In terms of generating new electronic information, fax has a minimal role. It is essentially a reprographic and transmission technology. It does not in itself create a new electronic version; it relies on there already being something available which needs to be transmitted elsewhere through the network. Fax publishing can therefore be excluded from the formats which are generating more information in electronic form.

Electronic books

Market size

Sony Data Discman
The Data Discman was launched in July 1990. Worldwide sales of Data Discman units were reported in March 1994 to be as follows:

Japan	over 200,000 units
USA	over 20,000 units
	(low price models)
Germany	over 20,000 units
	(some high price)
France	over 9,250 units
	(September 1993)
UK over	2,500 units

The focus since its inception has been on the consumer rather than scholarly or professional markets, though some migration may follow as the number of players becomes more widespread later in the decade.

Some of the titles planned for HEB (Handheld Electronic Books) are also suitable for existing CD-ROM installations. There are projections of between 200,000 and 700,000 Sega CD-ROM drives alone by the end of 1993. There is certainly a massive market interest in leisure-based CD-ROMs with recent press releases indicating that there have been as many CD deliveries in the last quarter of 1993 in the USA as in the first three-quarters together.

Products

Sony Data Discman
There is a complex array of handheld electronic books in existence. By far the most developed is the Sony Data Discman series. Most (but not all) electronic books come as handheld devices which play a CD-ROM containing the 'content' of the book. Each such book can hold up to 200 Mb of digital data (100,000 pages of text, 32,000 graphics or 6 hours of digital audio). The devices are powered by batteries and have headphone and TV connections.

Versions of the Data Discman include: the DD10-BZ (£399); DD10-EX (£299); DD-8 (£199) and DD-DR1 (£199). Other newer versions include DD-20 (multimedia electronic book player with built-in speakers), and the DD -30DBZ (multimedia book with computer connection). Prices are in the range of £200 to £400, including a number of bundled titles.

Sony's Data Discman is the pioneer of this development. Several manufacturers produce such players including Sony themselves, Sanyo, Sharp and Panasonic. They all adopt the same standard. The Data Discman uses a standard set of five easy methods of searching for information—Word search, Endword Search, Keyword Search, Multisearch and Graphic Search.

New versions are being announced which couple a handheld device and interchangeable CD discs. One of the latest is the PlayEBXA from Electronic Book Publishing Ltd, which allows a 3.5" CD-ROM to be played back through the Data Discman, laptop computers and IBM and Mac systems.

Number of titles

There are over 300 Data Discman titles now in publication. Most are reference works of particular appeal to the mobile businessman. Travel guides and dictionaries are popular products. For example, the breakdown of the 32 French titles is as follows:

Dictionaries	6 titles
Translation devices	5 titles
Practical guides	17 titles
Educational games	4 titles

It is the business market rather than the consumer market which is stimulating production of the titles available, particularly in the UK where there are no major high street stockists of the Data Discman.

Some 60 titles are published in the USA. A list of UK titles suitable for the Data Discman is given in Appendix 3 (33 titles). There are electronic book committees in 17 countries to promote Data Discman.

In the UK the lack of new titles to match original expectations has been variously attributed to the timing of major electronic book (EB) promotions, and to the unwillingness of Sony financially to support new titles. Some feel that the long-term potential of the electronic book is being eroded by short-term inadequacies in support and distribution.

There are some 60 members of the forum which promotes electronic books in the UK (Electronic Book Committee). Withdrawal of Columbia Tristar as a title publisher had a depressing effect on the development of titles in the UK; there were only some 34 titles in October 1993, despite all the initial hype.

Distribution

The whole business of electronic books on CD geared to the leisure and personal market seems to be taking off in the USA (see above). Even bookstores are showing an interest in marketing electronic titles in parallel with hard copies. This is not so in the UK where only Dillons seems to have shown any interest in stocking EB titles on a test basis.

Figure 85: *Worldwide hardware market*

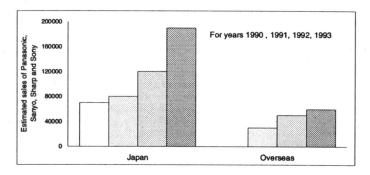

Estimated sales of Panasonic, Sanyo, Sharp and Sony

Figure 86: *Worldwide electronic book titles*

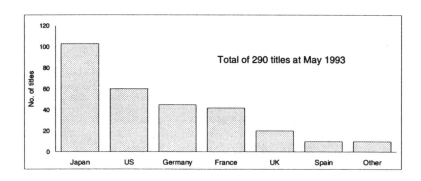

Market developments

There was considerable initial euphoria when the Data Discman was released in 1990. This has not been translated into actual unit sales. The reasons lie in the general malaise affecting the electronic industry worldwide in the early 1990's. Also, some of the problems were felt to be due to the high initial sales price of the playing unit, since adjusted downwards in the autumn of 1993 and involving a relaunch.

In general it is unlikely that there will be much immediate action on the electronic book front through to 2003.

References

Association of American Universities (1994) *Report of the task force on intellectual property rights in an electronic environment.* Research Libraries Project. Washington, DC: Association of American Universities.

Brown, D.J. (1993) A review of future developments in interlibrary loan and document delivery. *Information UK Outlooks*, **3**, Dec 1993.

Consulting Trust GmbH (1993) *New Opportunities for Publishers in the Information Services Market*, EUR 14925 EN, January 1993.

East, H. (1991) *Balancing the books: resourcing electronic information services in academic and public libraries.* CCIS Policy Paper 3. British Library R&D Report 6057. London: Centre for Communication and Information Studies.

East, H. and Vogel, S. (1991) *Indicators and revenues of database production and hosting in the United Kingdom.* Research paper.

Fishwick, F. (1993) *Book Trade Yearbook 1993.* London: Publishers Association.

Follett Review (1993) *Joint Funding Councils' Libraries Review Group: Report.* (Chairman: Sir Brian Follett). Bristol: HEFCE.

IMO Reviews. Information Market Observatory (IMO), Reports on specific new media developments in Europe. EU DG13, Luxembourg.

Laukamm, T. (1993) *New opportunities for publishers in the information services market.* Executive summary and background papers. EUR 14925. January and February 1993.

Meadows, J. (1995) Electronic publishing and the humanities. In *Networking in the humanities*, ed. S. Kenna and S. Ross. British Library Research. London: Bowker Saur.

Oakeshott, P. (1994) *Trends in journal subscriptions 1992*. London: The Publishers Association.

Odlyzko, A. (1995) Tragic loss or good riddance? The impending demise of traditional scholarly journals. *International Journal of Human-Computer Studies* (in press). Condensed version in *Notices of the American Mathematical Society*, January 1995. Available from ftp://netlib.att.com/netlib/att.math.odlyzko/tragic.loss

Rowland, F., McKnight, C. and Meadows, J. (eds) (1995) *Project ELVYN: an experiment in electronic journal delivery—facts, figures and findings*. British Library Research. London: Bowker Saur.

de Solla Price, D. (1963) *Little Science, Big Science*. Columbia University Press.

TFPL (1993) *Directory of CD-ROMs and Multimedia*. London: TFPL.

TFPL (1995) *The CD-ROM Directory 1995*. Ninth edition. London: TFPL.

Williams, M. (1993) The state of databases today. Reprinted in *Cuadra Directory of Databases*. Chicago.

SECTION D

Integrated forecasts of established and new scholarly media

There is a tide in the affairs of men,
Which, taken at the flood, leads on to fortune;
Omitted, all the voyage of their life
Is bound in shallows and in miseries.
William Shakespeare, 'Julius Caesar', IV.iii.218.

Overview

It is impossible to predict the date or speed of transition to systems such as those outlined in the previous section, mainly because they will be determined by social factors. The technology necessary for future systems is either already available or will be available within a few years. The speed with which these new technologies are adopted will depend on how quickly scholars are prepared to break with traditional methods in favour of novel and unfamiliar systems. A driving force in this will be how rapidly tenure and promotion committees accept electronic publications as having equal standing with print journals.

As Ann Okerson of ARL commented to Australian librarians:

Existing journals have a certain kind of process, have workers used to certain types of editing and production, have readers and writers who are accustomed to a certain way of doing things. They have a certain kind of management and mindset, perhaps. The new medium asks for a different skill set in production, a willingness to risk in a new format with few rules and standards, and readers who are agile (on the Internet, but equally applicable with the other new medium) or can be persuaded to be. Moving

existing titles into an electronic base and distributing them requires re-tooling and re-thinking of the procedures and outcomes
of publishing and can be financially risky.

The following charts represent a summary of the extrapolations which
can be made of the individual sectors to the year 2003, based purely on
the background data given in the previous sections.

Estimates are shown for each of the main types of new media where
an extrapolation is both possible and useful. The estimates for future
years are, of course, highly speculative. Technological forecasting remains an inexact art. In this particular case the difficulties are com-
pounded by the sheer variety of market dynamics which are in evidence.
The information industry could go any which way: pulled on one side
by the inherent conservatism of the individual researcher; pulled on the
other by the claimed efficiencies of the new technologies, together with
some killer 'applications'.

In starting out on this exercise to provide clarity on the information
scene to the year 2003, it was hoped that a single answer or set of ratios
between alternative traditional and new media would emerge. This has
not been possible. The data have been collected, the analysis has been
made, and the following section provides an integration of some of these
forecasts according to a consistent procedure. But in the final analysis
the only forecast that can be made is that in all likelihood there will be a
rich and variable harvest of new media available within the next ten
years, and that the impact on the book or journal could equally well be
peripheral or terminal, depending on prevailing social factors.

This is the start of a process of technological forecasting in this
important area of scientific communication, and it is hoped that better
data and better models will enable this process to be taken further in
future years.

Demography

This report has dwelt on the basic business tenets of publishing, notably
that none of the new media options can survive if there is insufficient
market size to be shared around.

Figure 87 is but one chart which demonstrates this market stability.
This particular chart shows that there is expected to be a static market
for students in the UK. After a period of dramatic growth in the late 1980s
we are witnessing a period of consolidation. It is unlikely that the next

wave of expansion in students numbers will be sufficient to drive up the market for academic publishing. And even if student numbers do grow by 2000, there may be further demographic changes as mature students become more important, numbers of part-time students increase, and international exchanges proliferate.

It would be a dangerous miscalculation to assume that the past numbers as well as past structural trends in the underlying market drivers will continue as a straight line into the future. A broader economic, social and political agenda has to be considered. Within this the academic and research sectors will be accommodated with other more significant social priorities—as wisps caught in the wind, driven into a new scientific ethic which, in turn, will have repercussions on the funding available for the various competitive printed and electronic communication formats.

Figure 87: *Changes in UK student numbers*

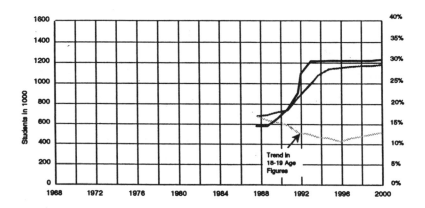

Printed publications

There will always be a requirement for the printed page. The conservatism of the academic and research communities is a factor in this, although it is a declining one as the new generation of Nintendo and Sega experts go through the ranks of higher education. But whilst this conservative group may be a declining portion of the scientists in the western world, there will always be a demand from the 'have not' nations of the world whose access to sophisticated computer and telecommunications equipment, let alone electricity, will remain minimal. Financial factors alone will continue to support a printed academic publishing sector.

The number of books and journal titles will continue to grow (Figure 88), driven on by the nature of science itself (the 'twigging phenomenon'). The 7 per cent overall growth in journal titles may slacken but long-term historical projections dictate that growth will continue along the lines shown below in Figure 89.

Figure 88: Printed scholarly books

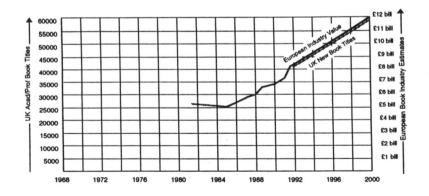

Figure 89: *Printed journals*

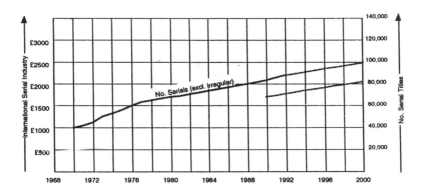

What these growth factors conceal is the incorporation of electronics within the publication process. Not only will costs be saved as more and more texts are received in machine readable form from authors (thereby reducing current typesetting charges), but there will be more scope for formatting the same publication in a variety of ways through the mechanism of creating a standard (SGML formatted, neutral) database. Both these cost saving trends may go some way to counteract the loss of some of the profitable print markets to the lower margins of electronic publishing.

Electronic documents

Although there is an assumed 'life cycle' to electronic document delivery, with the process of sending copies of documents being replaced by the source document itself stored as a digital file, the decline phase of the cycle may not occur with any real impact before 2003. Therefore we will still see some growth in this process.

Figure 90 illustrates several things. Firstly, it indicates that basic interlibrary resource sharing will continue at the same general growth as before, and, along with formal document delivery systems, will still dominate the main part of the separates business. However, on top of these traditional processes we see the emergence of new activities. These include the so-called CAS-IAS activities (current alerting service combined with individual article supply) and the continued importance of commercial document suppliers, albeit operating from a small base of activity at present. 'Personal purchases', whereby individuals use credit cards and deposit accounts to buy articles on demand, may also prove to be a growing activity, particularly as selective dissemination of information (SDI) against a profile of researcher's interests gathers pace after some false starts.

Figure 90: *Document delivery traffic*

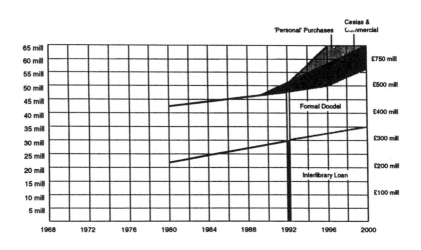

Bibliographic databases

There is an historical trend which can be mapped out and extrapolated into the future to give a best fit estimate of the numbers of online searches in the USA from the late 1970s to the early 1990s (Figure 91).

Figure 91: Bibliographic databases

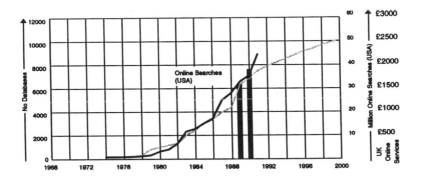

Online industry

The value of the UK online information industry alone can also be plotted. (The industry values are in million of pounds sterling.) Figure 92 includes the databases and the vendors of the databases, both bibliographic and real-time financial. Figures up to 1992 are actual (or as accurate as is possible). Beyond that they involve a straightline projection.

Figure 92: UK online industry, 1988-2000 (in £ mil)

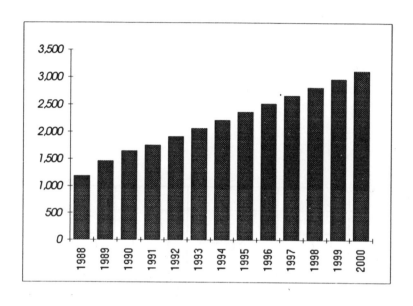

Videotex services

Videotex in the UK has had a mixed history. The initial wave of enthusiasm for Prestel in the mid 1970s waned as the consumer market failed to take off, and in 1994 British Telecom finally withdrew even from the business sector, leaving videotex services in the hands of a few private clients. (The situation is entirely different in France where the Minitel system has been responsible for driving the database industry, and 5.3 million inexpensive terminals have provided a fertile infrastructure.)

Figure 93 shows the growth of videotex terminals in the UK, according to figures given in the *EP Journal* (1993). The data for 1995 and 2000 are approximations based on historical trends.

Figure 93: Growth of videotex services in the UK (number of terminals)

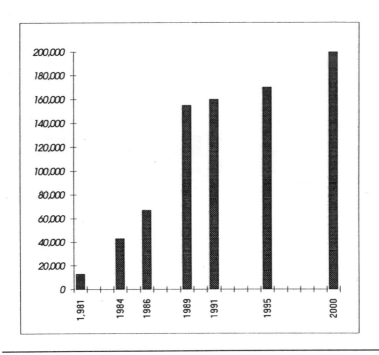

Audiotex services

Figure 94 shows the growth in revenues (in millions of pounds sterling) in the audiotex services in the UK. The 1994 figure is an estimate (source: Association of Telephone and Information and Entertainment Providers, *Guide to the premium rate and automatic answering industry*). Estimates are based on the industry figures up to 1993. Thereafter the assumed 10-11 per cent recent growth in the 'mature' UK market for audiotex will continue, though it should be pointed out that very little of this relates to scholarly information. Most is geared to the consumer information, sport and entertainment sectors.

Figure 94: UK premium rate service revenues (in million £)

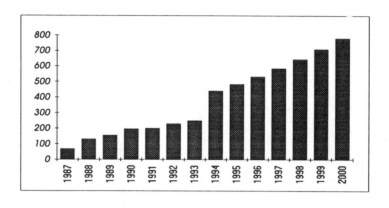

Optical publishing

Here we enter the realms of staggering recent growth and exaggerated promises for the future. If the forecasts and projections bear fruit, then the world sales of CD would soon surpass that of the printed book and journals industries combined. Even a more realistic extrapolation still suggests that CD-ROM would become a dominant publishing format by 2000 (Figure 95).

This assumes that the networks do not detract from the CD-ROM market. Many experts believe that CD-ROM is a transient technology for electronic publishing and that it will not be able to withstand the competition from real-time online database access through the Internet and the emerging superhighways, particularly as these will allow multi-media data provision—a real 'value-added' over printed options.

CD-Interactive (CD-I), one of a series of advanced CD applications, is also forecast to grow at astonishing rates (Figure 96).

Figure 95: CD-ROM

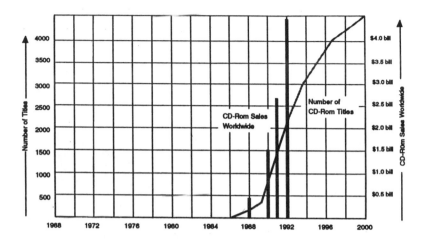

Figure 96: CD-Interactive

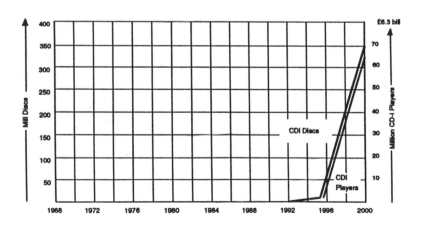

Total information industry

The growth in the various print-based forms of information in the next few years is shown in Figure 97.

***Figure 97**: Print-based information systems*

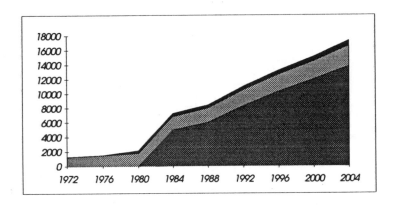

Books represent the main base of the graph, then serials, and document delivery a growing but still small element on top. It should be recognized that these are international figures, and the books component takes in all forms of books, particularly those aimed at the consumer market.

The total UK printed and electronic publishing industry to 2002/3 is shown in Figure 98. The various sectors are, from the bottom upwards:

- Books (all forms)
- Serials/Journals (STM)
- Document Delivery
- Online databases and Hosts (including financial)
- Videotex
- Audiotex
- Optical (CD-ROM)
- CD-I

Figure 98: *Total UK printed and electronic publishing industry to 2002/3 (figures in £ mil)*

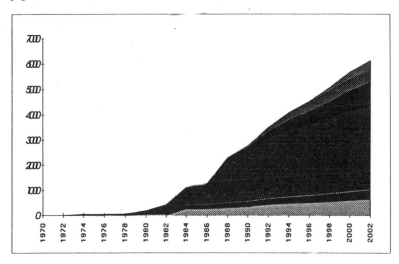

Against this growth, the Demand Line would remain static at the 1990-1992 level (in real terms) indicating that the potential for all media formats to achieve their respective goals in the UK is limited (Figure 99).

Figure 99: *Balance of traditional and new media publications during the 1990s*

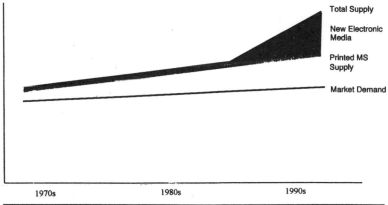

References

EP Journal (1993) **7**(1), April/May, 4. London: Electronic Publishing Services Ltd.

SECTION E

Legal deposit issues

This report demonstrates that the legal deposit of electronic publications will present the scholarly community with complex problems. Legal deposit within the British Library at present ensures that the Library receives a copy of 'every book published in the United Kingdom', under the provisions of section 15 of the Copyright Act of 1911. The definition of 'book' includes 'every part or division of a book, pamphlet, sheet of letterpress, sheet of music, map, plan, chart or table separately published but...not...any subsequent edition unless [it] contains additions or alterations'. The legal deposit requirements therefore encompass all forms of publishing, from research material through to fiction and children's books.

This report recognizes the diverse coverage of legal deposit but looks at the specific challenges affecting the scientific, technical and medical publications in particular. It does not pretend that legal deposit is of concern solely to this area, merely that this area poses unique market/technological/commercial constraints which should be taken into consideration in evaluating such material, and which may therefore have more general repercussions in other areas.

Another issue in relation to electronic publishing is presented by the British Library's basic remit. The British Library was established by the 1972 Act as a 'national centre for reference, study and bibliographical and other information services, in relation to both to scientific and technological matters and to the humanities'. This service should consist of a 'comprehensive collection of books, manuscripts, periodicals, films and other recorded matter, whether printed or otherwise'. To accomplish this task the British Library can collect the UK published material by virtue of legal deposit (filled in where necessary with purchases of duplicated or missing items) but also has to buy and maintain a great deal of material published overseas. This applies to non-English language publications as well.

These two requirements—the one created by section 15 of the 1911

Copyright Act to receive published enhancements from UK sources under legal deposit, and the other by the British Library mandate to provide a comprehensive information service—are complementary but not synonymous. The one requires a focus on the attentions of the UK publishing industry and the other on the information industry on a global scale.

The data collected in this report show the extent of the problem facing the British Library. The biggest problem is how to adapt the policies of the Library to cope with the fact that the form of 'publication' is changing dramatically from that envisaged in the 1911 Copyright and the 1972 British Library Acts. 'Information' is no longer a product which can be felt, handled and shelved. It increasingly exists on the airwaves, disseminated around the world in nanoseconds through networks which have few physical characteristics.

How does one apply a legal deposit provision to a bulletin board? And yet these boards are the embryos of a new information system which potentially displaces some of the functionality of the scholarly information process. As such they require, for the British Library's mission to be fulfilled, to be brought within its service provision. How does one decide whether a CD-ROM which incorporates a new search and retrieval method is new material (a new edition) or is only a reformatting of information already acquired under legal deposit? Many scholarly journal publishers are preparing to launch CD-ROM versions of their journal titles for archival purposes—should these be included under legal deposit?

The delicate nature of these and many other related decisions means that legal deposit and British Library acquisitions policies have to be reviewed again in the light of the variety of changes which are taking place in the scholarly publishing area.

This report has assembled some background to these deliberations. It goes back to the basic problem which faces the scholarly publishing process, that there is an irreconcilable split between the forces which create the Supply of scholarly information and those which satisfy the Demand. Given this distinction, the pressures involved in each are looked at in depth.

The conclusion from this approach is that the late 1990s will see chaos in the formal publishing system of scholarly journals, and the demise of the learned monograph. The market forces are leading to lower sales, and the market will be further weakened by the appearance of a wide variety of new media products aimed at groups and sections of the research community, each new medium claiming unique value-added features. The outcome will inevitably be a downsizing of the present sales levels of books and journals, forcing all but the core publications into financial collapse.

The 1911 provisions for legal deposit are increasingly out of date as new forms of information services appear, produced by groups which are not necessarily from the old school of print-on-paper publishing, and using formats which were never conceived by the policy makers who wrote and passed the Act. This report describes some of the forecasts being made for the new services, and illustrates their separate forecasts and extrapolations in a consistent form.

It has been shown that more 'publications' will be available, serving an international community with a wider variety of forms. As part of its remit the British Library will be expected to acquire and make available many of these new publishing forms, although many will be 'duplicates' in terms of editorial content.

The real challenge will be to adapt the Library's remit to take into account the fact that the commercial and marketing pressures building up within the system are creating problems of their own. Library policy for the future needs to take account of these problems—of static R&D funding, of more pressure for higher education in the UK without additional teaching staff, of new optical storage devices which have achieved great popularity, of network communications within the world of the Internet—which directly influence the form which the information industry will take in the year 2000 and beyond. Legal deposit legislation and the BL remit need to be set within this new framework.

This is why the report pays so much attention to infrastructural issues. If the infrastructure changes, then the objectives of the national library cannot effectively be achieved through a minor adjustment and tinkering process. The policy has to be brought within the real world of commercial life, which at present is far from stable.

SECTION F

Requirement for data and economic models

The information industry is bedevilled by the lack of data in an integrated form on market size and trends. This is plainly evident from the audit of surveys looked at and used in the course of this research. While the EU Information Market Observatory collects some data, and forecasts are generated by a number of consultancy groups, these are usually with a particular industry sector in mind. They fail to make effective comparisons with other information industry sectors against which they compete for supply and market share, with the consequence that much exaggeration of the market potential for specific sectors occurs.

There is only one pot of gold accessible to all the publications, both traditional and new media, namely the institutional library. Unless and until the 'end user' becomes an active buyer of material using money which does not go into the library at present, then the future of all forms of publishing will be constrained by the static size of this pot. One of the requirements for a flourishing information industry therefore is to increase this pot of gold. The Follett review (1993) provides no immediate solace in this direction.

Given this situation the library may find it increasingly hard to maintain service because of reducing support and funding, and may be obliged to seek full cost recovery for services supplied. The 'public good' function of national libraries will be a subject for discussion (Martyn *et al.*, 1990). Already there are chinks appearing in the Document Supply service and its traditional policy of not paying royalties. (Even if it did pay royalties across the board, it would not solve some of the more basic problems facing STM journal publishing which are identified in this report.)

The implications for the commercial basis of traditional and electronic publishing need further exploration. The ecology of information dissemination is delicately balanced, and if one part gets out of step it will have serious consequences on other parts (for example, excessive document delivery destroying the source journals; electronic publishing making printed publishing commercially unattractive). We need effective and acceptable econometric models.

Many pundits remain convinced at heart that off-line publishing is likely to be more attractive than online in the short to medium term. Print will remain supreme in the media mix for many years to come because of its convenience, portability and familiarity, but that does not mean it will be financially rewarding. And this is the rub—that no matter how conservative and cautious we feel the end user will be about throwing out the book, there are new and powerful forces (organizations and technology) which have a different agenda and it is these which are changing the way information will be created and disseminated.

This report skates over the surface of many fundamental issues. Accurate data collection in particular is required, and the broad 'database' included in this survey needs to be refined, updated and integrated into relevant models. It is hoped that this will be done with a sense of priority and urgency. Only then can the debate on the role and operations of printed publishing be conducted within a commercial as well as a strictly bibliographic context.

References

Follett Review (1993) *Joint Funding Councils' Libraries Review Group: Report*. (Chairman: Sir Brian Follett). Bristol: HEFCE.

Martyn, J., Vickers, P., and Feeney, M. (eds.) (1990) *Information UK 2000*. London: Bowker Saur.

SECTION G

Conclusions and recommendations

This report demonstrates that forecasting the future of electronic publications is bedevilled by interaction of a wide variety of relevant factors. Each has its own objectives and timetable; to bring them together into an integrated single forecast and provide a description of what the information industry will look like in the year 2003 is a challenge. One method is to extrapolate the forecasts for each of the new media, using forecasts of the printed publications as a benchmark. This technique suffers from the exuberance of those focusing on just one technology in isolation as providing the ultimate salvation to the scientific communication process.

There is a life cycle to each new technology (and its information-related applications). The birth and development phases show rapid growth; at some stage each new technology and the services it spawns reach market maturity. Thereafter it declines as it makes way for the even newer and more effective technologies. The science information industry is at the start of the period when a whole range of new technologies are about to make an impact on the dissemination process. Computer-based publishing (on floppy discs), competes with network-based publishing (through the Internet) and optical-based publishing (CD-ROM), and all will vie with multimedia forms of publishing which can make use of a variety of base technologies. The upshot is that there is an unholy scramble for market positioning. All this is taking place now, in the mid-1990s.

Each technology/information application has its advocates suggesting that the birth and developmental phases of the cycle will be steeper and last longer than others. Putting all their forecasts together produces an untenable macro-level picture. It would lead to more being spent on dissemination than is generated by the research community.

This is one of the key conclusions of this report— that each forecast for any new information medium within scientific communication has to take into account the whole integrated picture. It has to be related to its ability to survive, not only against the challenge from print publishing, but also from other new electronic and optical-based services. There is only one single 'pot of gold'. This will be split into ever increasing ladles as the efficiencies of more and more new media applications come to market.

This has one serious commercial consequence; except for a few 'winners', many of the other new media will never achieve the potential which is being claimed for them because of the intense media competition, and the 'downsizing' of market sizes which will occur. A constant pot of gold; many new media and applications competing for it; the result is an overall business which will become increasingly unprofitable. (We may be seeing the first signs of such a shakeout with the inability of the much-hyped 'handheld electronic book' to sustain the course. A similar case could be made for electronic document delivery.)

A concern which comes through the report is that if this complex interaction of new media takes place before a commercial rationale for the dissemination of scientific research results can be found, then the main victim would be Science itself. At present the research community is well served by the established print products of book and journal. Downsizing of the market to accommodate the new media could destroy the commercial fabric of the print system before an electronic (or alternative) new media publishing system is in place and commercially sustainable.

All this presupposes that the 'pot of gold' is finite. If there are signs that this could increase then some of the bleak assumptions about the commercial basis for scientific communication made above could be ill-founded.

The section dealing with 'Demand' issues investigates the ability of the market size (or funds to buy research results) to increase. The main organizational entity which is the funnel for much of the funds to support scientific information flow is the research library. There are no indications that other funding sources will be awakened by the challenges resulting from the emerging new electronic era. Payment by individuals from personal funds seems to be locked up as an issue— existing surveys indicate that they are unwilling to spend anything more than the costs of a few trade magazine subscriptions out of their own pockets. Departmental and research projects could yield some increase in funds to supplement the pot of gold, but only to a peripheral extent.

A further conclusion from this study is that the 'Supply' and the 'Demand' forces for scientific information are and will continue to be out of step. The supply of publishable information is partly a response to a continued national and economic commitment to R&D, and that this is between 2 per cent and 3 per cent of a developed nation's gross national product. It is also a response to the need for academic researchers to gain prestige, international recognition, and further funding—the 'publish or perish' syndrome, still as appropriate today as it was a decade ago. The demand factors are dictated at a local level, usually within a research institute, university or organization. Financial officers make the decision on how much money flows into the library pot based on the extent of competition for local resources. Within academia in particular the library has lost out and seen its percentage share of campus funds fall. No amount of recourse to claims that the 'citadel of learning' is being tarnished by this process can overcome the hard nosed reality that the cost/benefits of investing in a library are unproven and unquantifiable.

Potential salvation could come if the forces which were behind the national research effort were to grow to such an extent that the library returns to the halcyon days of the early 1970s when their budgets were less impoverished. If there were to be a growth in the population which could sustain an expanding research community then this might trickle through to enable the library to benefit from such expansion of demand (albeit supply of information as well). The demographic picture is not propitious. The developed world will see a static population in general, with the growth coming in the developing world. Such growth in the latter will not feed through to a growth in the gross national product upon which research is based. Even if it did, there is still a 'take-off' period before research becomes an ingrained part of the national resource commitment. In the case of the developing world there is also a cultural barrier against science and research to overcome, one which has become less of a handicap within the developed world.

Higher education support and R&D expenditures are also derived from this basic demographic position. No major expansion in the overall R&D effort can be expected given the current socio-political climate worldwide.

What is more likely to occur is a shift in priorities between disciplines. Basic research is being made less of a focus, with 'near market applications' being the aim of much research work in industry and now increasingly within academia. Megascience projects also drain funds from some of the more specialized research areas as large international teams cooperate to break new technological frontiers. Multidisciplinary science is also emerging to provide a common approach to solving an identifiable social issue. Whereas the pot of gold for science communication remains constant, there are dynamic forces at play which change the nature of the research effort.

To repeat the statement made at the beginning of this summary, there are stresses and strains within the scientific system which makes it difficult to be positive about the scenario facing the information community in the year 2003. This report explores some of the background issues but finds the challenge of the commitment to producing one final figure or ratio too daunting.

What is proposed instead is that more effort is made to collect relevant data and feed it into proven economic models to enable librarians and publishers to meet the various technological and social challenges in a quantifiable way during the next decade. Failure to provide the necessary commitment to this concept could lead to many existing players drifting rudderless into unknown and uncharted waters. A long-term vision, however vague that vision is, towards which the organization can strive would appear to be a necessary requisite given the dynamics and flux within the current scientific information industry.

BIBLIOGRAPHY AND READING LIST

Strategic forecasts

Laukamm, T., *New opportunities for publishers in the information services market*. Executive summary and background papers. EUR 14925. January and February 1993.

Brown, D.J., *Electronic Publishing and Libraries: planning for the impact and growth to 2003*. British Library Research. London: Bowker-Saur, 1996.

Background statistics

Unesco, *Unesco Statistical Handbook 1992*. Paris: Unesco Publishing, 1992

Unesco, *World Science Report 1993*. Paris: Unesco Publishing, 1993.

User studies

Royal Society, British Library and Association of Learned and Professional Society Publishers, *The scientific, technical and medical information system in the UK*. British Library R&D Report 6123. London: The Royal Society, 1993.

Schauder, D., Electronic publishing of professional articles: attitudes of academics and implications for the scholarly communication industry. *Journal of the American Society for Information Science*, **45**(2), 1994, 73-100.

Statistical overview of information products

Information Market Observatory (IMO), *Reports on specific new media developments in Europe*. EU DG13, Luxembourg.

Bibliographic databases

Williams, M., The state of databases today. Reprinted in *Cuadra Directory of Databases*. Chicago,1993.

East, H. and Vogel, S., *Indicators and revenues of database production and hosting in the United Kingdom*. CCIS Research Paper. London: Centre for Communication and Information Studies, 1991.

East, H. and Tilson, Y., *The liberated enduser: developments in practice and policy for database provision to the academic community*. CCIS Policy Paper No. 4, July 1993. London: University of Westminster, 1993.

CD publications

TFPL, *The CD-ROM Directory 1995*. Ninth edition. London: TFPL, 1995.

Heijne M., Survey of projects and services in document delivery (version 3). SURFnet, bv, February 1994.

Brown, D.J., A review of future developments in interlibrary loan and document delivery. *Information UK Outlooks*, **3**, Dec 1993.

Network publishing

Electronic Publishing Services, *Network publishing: a multi client study*. London, December 1992.

Association of Research Libraries, *Directory of Electronic Journals, Newsletters and Academic Discussions Lists*. Washington, DC: Association of Research Libraries, Office of Scientific and Academic Publishing, May 1994.

Moderated update of new e-journals from ejrnl@uacsc2.albany.edu

Electronic preprints

Odlyzko, A., Tragic loss or good riddance? The impending demise of traditional scholarly journals. *International Journal of Human-Computer Studies* (in press). Condensed version in *Notices of the American*

Mathematical Society, January 1995. Available from ftp://netlib.att.com/netlib/att.math.odlyzko/tragic.loss

Harnad, S., Scholarly skywriting and the prepublication continuum of scientific inquiry. *Psychological Science*, **1**, 1990, 342-344.

Multimedia

The multimedia yearbook 1995, London: Interactive Media Publications, 1995.

Information industry assessments

Grycz, C. (ed.), Special issue on economic models. *Networked Information Serials Review*, **18**(1-2), 1992.

Information industry factbook. The Information Industry Association's Report. Stamford, Conn: Digital Information Group, 1988 and 1989/90 editions.

Science and engineering indicators—1993. Washington DC: National Science Board, 1994.

Cultural trends 1992: books, libraries and reading. Issue 16. London: Policy Studies Institute, 1992.

INA directory of UK networked services. British Library R&D Report No. 6175. London: The British Library, 1994.

Cox, J., The changing role of the subscription agent. *Learned Publishing*, **5**(4), 1992, 205.

Library statistics

Association of Research Libraries, *Report of the ARL serials project*. Washington, DC: Association of Research Libraries, 1989.

Follett Review, *Joint Funding Councils' Libraries Review Group: Report*. (Chairman: Sir Brian Follett). Bristol: HEFCE, 1993.

UKOLN, *Libraries and IT: working papers of the information technology sub-committee of the HEFC's Libraries Review*. Bath: UKOLN, 1993.

Association of Research Libraries, *Association of Research Libraries*

(ARL) Statistics. Washington, DC: Association of Research Libraries, 1992.

Vickers, P. and Martyn, J., The impact of electronic publishing on library services in the UK: report of the British Library working party on electronic publishing. LIR Report 102. London: The British Library, 1994.

Publisher statistics

Byrd, G. D., *An economic commons tragedy for research libraries: scholarly journal publishing and pricing trends.* College and Research Libraries conference, 1990.

Oakeshott, P., *Trends in Journal Subscriptions 1992.* London: The Publishers Association (SPE and CAPP), 1994.

Fishwick, F., *Book Trade Yearbook 1993.* London: The Publishers Association, 1993.

Appendices

Table 17: First degree graduates from UK universities

		1989	1990	1991	1992	1993	1994	1995
Medicine & dentistry	O	4223	4388	4395	4519	4373	4447	4551
	N	0	0	0	0	0	0	0
	Total	4223	4388	4395	4519	4373	4447	4551
Studies allied to medicine	O	1980	2104	2214	2339	2619	2992	3735
	N	769	806	862	1154	1531	1673	2452
	Total	2749	2910	3076	3493	4150	4665	6187
Biological sciences	O	5216	5597	5775	6328	6819	7605	8709
	N	841	777	862	860	1146	1240	1685
	Total	6057	6374	6637	7188	7965	8845	10394
Veterinary science, agriculture & related studies	O	1294	1251	1158	1182	1212	1196	1254
	N	16	88	151	254	365	509	573
	Total	1310	1339	1309	1436	1577	1705	1827
Physical sciences	O	6054	6336	6302	6988	7355	7972	8586
	N	1214	1333	1655	2148	2399	3001	3630
	Total	7268	7669	7957	9136	9754	10973	12216
Mathematical sciences	O	4519	4572	5195	5634	5725	6064	6353
	N	1783	2056	2422	3043	4096	4341	5536
	Total	6302	6628	7617	8677	9821	10405	11889
Engineering & technology	O	9349	9662	9485	9829	10650	11177	11175
	N	4133	4614	4832	5297	5728	6444	7218
	Total	13482	14276	14317	15126	16378	17621	18393
Architecture & related studies	O	987	1098	977	1256	1371	1395	1418
	N	1910	1973	2282	2678	3170	3468	4207
	Total	2897	3071	3259	3934	4541	4863	5625
Social sciences	O	12518	12482	12615	13106	13643	14856	16486
	N	5663	5922	6407	7093	7908	9217	11072
	Total	18181	18404	19022	20199	21551	24073	27558
Business & financial studies	O	3661	4150	4179	4391	4669	5183	5961
	N	4460	5001	6642	7790	9328	10845	13516
	Total	8121	9151	10821	12181	13997	16028	19477
Librarianship & info. science	O	127	101	152	186	224	273	322
	N	576	677	689	720	060	1118	1239
	Total	703	778	841	906	1284	1391	1561
Languages & related studies	O	7708	7701	7823	8382	8796	10140	10923
	N	1140	1247	1467	1578	1882	2129	2359
	Total	8848	8948	9290	9960	10678	12269	13282
Humanities	O	5094	5131	5262	5881	6393	7034	7875
	N	382	477	493	670	723	920	1061
	Total	5476	5608	5755	6551	7116	7954	8936
Creative arts	O	1367	1400	1265	1388	1525	1656	1722
	N	3178	3496	3799	4290	4758	5534	6292
	Total	4545	1896	5064	5678	6283	7190	8014
Education	O	1167	1309	1393	1359	1610	1760	1857
	N	1996	2370	2734	3016	3507	3709	4307
	Total	3163	3679	4127	4375	5117	5469	6164
Multi-disciplinary studies	O	8377	8689	9259	9573	9961	10692	12420
	N	5189	5664	6631	7703	9613	11737	14288
	Total	13566	14353	15890	17276	19574	22429	26708
TOTALS	O	73641	75971	77449	82341	86945	94442	103347
	N	33250	36501	41928	48294	57214	65885	79435
	Total	106891	112472	119377	130635	144159	160327	182782

Table 18: Scientific and technical personnel in R&D

Country	Year	Scientists	Technicians	Total
Austria	1984	7609	6817	14426
Belgium	1988	16646	20124	36770
Belarus	1988	44100	-	-
Bulgaria	1987	50585	11662	62247
Former				
Czechoslovakia	1989	65475	42876	108351
Denmark	1989	10662	14786	25448
Finland	1989	11317	9878	21195
France	1988	115163	167936	283099
Germany (GDR)	1989	127449	67624	195073
(FDR)	1987	165614	122458	288072
Greece	1986	534	488	1022
Hungary	1989	20431	14113	34544
Iceland	1989	773	404	1177
Ireland	1988	6351	1291	7642
Italy	1988	74833	38287	113120
Malta	1988	34	5	39
Netherlands	1988	37520	26900	64420
Norway	1989	12100	8600	20700
Poland	1989	32500	-	-
Portugal	1988	5004	3571	8575
Romania	1989	59670	42931	102601
San Marino	1986	-	- -	
Spain	1988	31170	9914	41084
Sweden	1987	22725	29086	51811
Switzerland	1989	9418	8916	18334

Table 19: International R&D expenditures

R&D Expenditures (billions of constant 1982 $)

	USA	Japan	W. Germany	France	UK	Italy	Sweden
1961	45.8	3.9	NA	3.2	8.1	NA	NA
1962	48.2	4.4	4.2	3.6	NA	NA	NA
1963	52.6	4.9	4.9	4.0	NA	1.5	NA
1964	57.2	5.5	5.8	5.0	8.4	NA	0.7
1965	59.4	6.1	6.7	5.8	NA	1.6	NA
1966	62.6	6.6	7.3	6.3	8.8	NA	NA
1967	64.4	7.6	7.9	6.8	8.9	2.0	0.8
1968	65.5	9.0	8.4	7.0	9.1	2.3	NA
1969	64.7	10.5	8.3	7.1	9.4	2.6	0.8
1970	62.4	12.6	10.1	7.5	NA	3.0	NA
1971	60.4	13.5	11.0	7.8	NA	3.1	1.1
1972	61.4	14.9	11.5	8.0	9.3	3.2	NA
1973	62.4	16.3	11.4	8.0	NA	3.3	1.2
1974	61.5	16.6	11.6	8.3	NA	3.2	NA
1975	59.9	16.8	12.0	8.3	10.1	3.5	1.4
1976	62.1	17.5	12.2	8.5	NA	3.4	NA
1977	63.7	18.2	12.5	8.7	NA	3.6	1.5
1978	66.8	19.3	13.5	9.0	11.1	3.5	NA
1979	70.1	21.2	15.2	9.6	NA	3.7	1.6
1980	73.3	23.4	15.5	9.9	NA	3.9	NA
1981	76.6	25.8	16.1	10.9	12.2	4.6	2.0
1982	80.0	27.7	16.5	11.7	NA	4.8	NA
1983	85.8	30.1	16.0	12.0	11.9	5.1	2.3
1984	93.8	32.6	17.0	12.7	NA	6.3	NA
1985	102.5	36.1	18.8	13.1	12.8	6.5	2.8
1986	104.9	36.5	19.3	13.3	13.5	7.1	NA
1987	106.6	39.1	20.2	13.8	13.6	8.2	3.0
1988	110.2	42.0	20.6	14.4	13.5	8.2	NA
1989	111.1	45.9	21.9	15.0	13.2		2.9

Source: Science Resources Studies Division, National Science

and R&D as a percentage of GNP: 1961-89

R&D Expenditures as % of GNP

USA	Japan	W. Germany	France	UK	Italy	Sweden
2.7	1.4	NA	1.4	2.5	NA	NA
2.7	1.5	1.2	1.5	NA	NA	NA
2.8	1.5	1.4	1.6	NA	0.6	NA
2.9	1.5	1.6	1.8	2.3	NA	1.2
2.8	1.6	1.7	2.0	NA	0.7	NA
2.8	1.5	1.8	2.1	2.3	NA	NA
2.8	1.6	2.0	2.2	2.3	0.7	1.3
2.8	1.7	2.0	2.1	2.2	0.8	NA
2.7	1.7	1.8	2.0	2.3	0.8	1.3
2.6	1.9	2.1	1.9	NA	0.9	NA
2.4	1.9	2.2	1.9	NA	0.9	1.5
2.4	1.9	2.2	1.9	2.1	0.9	NA
2.3	2.0	2.1	1.8	NA	0.8	1.6
2.2	2.0	2.1	1.8	NA	0.8	NA
2.2	2.0	2.2	1.8	2.1	0.9	1.7
2.2	2.0	2.1	1.8	NA	0.9	NA
2.2	2.0	2.1	1.8	NA	0.9	1.8
2.1	2.0	2.2	1.8	2.2	0.8	NA
2.2	2.1	2.4	1.8	NA	0.8	1.9
2.3	2.2	2.4	1.8	NA	0.9	NA
2.4	2.3	2.5	2.0	2.4	1.0	2.4
2.5	2.4	2.6	2.1	NA	1.1	NA
2.6	2.6	2.5	2.1	2.2	1.1	2.6
2.7	2.6	2.6	2.2	NA	1.0	NA
2.8	2.8	2.8	2.3	2.3	1.1	3.0
2.8	2.8	2.8	2.2	2.4	1.1	NA
2.8	2.8	2.9	2.3	2.3	1.2	3.0
2.7	2.9	2.9	2.3	2.2	1.3	NA
2.7	3.0	2.9	2.3	2.0	1.3	2.8

Foundation, International Science & Technology Data Update.

Table 20: *Science & Engineering graduate students,*

	1980	1981	1982	1983	1984
Physical sciences	26952	27382	28199	29466	30064
Mathematics	15360	15915	17199	17397	17478
Computer sciences	13578	16437	19812	23616	25810
Environmental sciences	14208	14422	15174	15544	15612
Life sciences	60144	59079	58624	58345	58233
Psychology	40636	40691	40082	41039	41074
Social sciences	81571	79654	77036	72203	70112
Total Sciences	252449	253580	256126	257610	258383
Total Engineering	75084	80479	84581	91937	93644
Total Science & Engineering	327533	334059	340707	349547	352027

by field, 1980-90

1985	1986	1987	1988	1989	1990
30995	32260	32738	32972	33628	34337
17613	17990	18573	19141	19382	19884
29844	31425	32137	32787	32846	34507
15545	15163	14522	14032	13848	14159
57918	58545	58456	59316	60655	62104
41308	41551	42888	44389	46304	48659
70548	70482	71674	71918	74569	78620
263771	267416	270988	274555	281232	292270
96951	103071	104644	103719	104815	109299
360722	370487	375632	378274	386047	401569

Table 21: *UK electronic book titles,Sept 1993*

Title	Publisher	Developer	Price
AA Guide to Hotels and Restaurants in Britain	Automobile Association	Attica	£30
Berlitz Basic French	Berlitz/Electronic Book Publishing	Electronic Book Publishing	£40
Berlitz Basic German	Berlitz/Electronic Book Publishing	Electronic Book Publishing	£40
Berlitz Basic Italian	Berlitz/Electronic Book Publishing	Electronic Book Publishing	£40
Berlitz Basic Spanish	Berlitz/Electronic Book Publishing	Electronic Book Publishing	£40
Berlitz Business Traveler	Berlitz/Electronic Book Publishing	Electronic Book Publishing	£35
Bluffer's Guide to Business	The Bluffer's Guides/ Attica Cybernetics	Attica	£30
Bluffer's Guide to High Society	The Bluffer's Guides/ Attica Cybernetics	Attica	£25
Chambers Science and Technology Library	Chambers/ Electronic Book Publishing	Electronic Book Publishing	£40
Collins Gem Electronic Food File	Collins/SEPC	Attica	£25
Concise Oxford Dictionary and Thesaurus	Oxford University Press/ Electronic Book Publishing	Electronic Book Publishing	£30
Dictionary of Business	Peter Collins/SEPC	Howard BLAYER	£30
Electronic Speechwriter's Kit	SEPC	Pocket Information	£30
Electronic TIME OUT 4 City Guide	Time Out/SEPC	Pocket Information	£30
Electronic TIME OUT London Guide	Time Out/SEPC	Pocket Information	£30
Financial Times Directory of European Companies	FT/SEPC Electronic Book Publishing	Electronic Book Publishing	£45
Harrap's Multilingual Dictionary	Harrap	SANSHUSHA	£30
Hoover's Handbook of American and World Business	Reference Press/ Electronic Book Publishing	Electronic Book Publishing	£45
Hugh Johnson's Wine Guide	Mitchell Beazley	Pocket Information	£30
Hutchinson's Encyclopedic Dictionary	Helicon	Attica	£30
Hutchinson's Gallup Info	Helicon	Pocket Information	£30
Hutchinson's Guide to the World	Helicon	Attica	£30
Joy of Sex	Mitchell Beazley	Pocket Information	£40
Listen and Read 1	Penguin	Pocket Information	£40
Listen and Read 2	Penguin	Pocket Information	£40
Listen and Read 3	Penguin	Pocket Information	£40
Listen and Read 4	Penguin	Pocket Information	£40
Listen and Read 5	Penguin	Pocket Information	£40
Official Scrabble Word Finder	Chambers/ Electronic Book Publishing	Electronic Book Publishing	£25
Our Environment: Saving the Planet	Electronic Book Publishing	Electronic Book Publishing	£27
Oxford Dictionary of Quotations	Oxford University Press/ Electronic Book Publishing	Electronic Book Publishing	£27
Thomson Electronic Directory	Thomson	Attica	£30

Abbreviations

ALPSP	Association of Learned and Professional Society Publishers
ARL	Association of Research Libraries
BLDSC	British Library Document Supply Centre
CAP c	omputer aided production
CAS	current awareness services
CCC	Copyright Clearance Center
CD-I	Compact Disc-Interactive
CD-ROM	Compact Disc-Read Only Memory
CERN	Centre Européene de Recherche Nucléaire
CLA	Copyright Licensing Agency
CORE	Chemistry Online Retrieval Experiment
DTD	Document Type Definition
EPS	Encapsulated PostScript
EU	European Union
GDP	gross domestic product
GNP	gross national product
HEB	handheld electronic books
HEI	higher education institutions
IAS	individual article supply
IT	information technology
LANs	local area networks
NSF	National Science Foundation
OINC	'out in the cold'
PLS	Publishers Licensing Society
R&D	research and development
SDI	selective dissemination of information
SGML	Standard Generalized Markup Language
TCP/IP	Transmission Control Protocol/Internet Protocol
TIFF	Tagged Image File Format
USP	unique selling points

Index

abstracts
CD-ROMS 44
printed journals 54
access strategy
inter-library loans 92, 94
university libraries 41
applied research versus basic research 21, 30, 173
articles *see* research articles
Association of Research Libraries 41-2
audiotex
Europe 133
Japan 133
market size 133, 159, 160*fig*
subjects 133

balancing supply and demand 2
basic research versus applied research 21, 30, 173
bibliographic databases
Europe 105*fig*
growth rate 106-8, 157*fig*
market size 104-6
number of records 108*fig*
production
1975-1992 107*fig*
1991 106*fig*
United Kingdom 112
usage 108-9
see also online searching
biologists, use of networks 48*fig*
book publishing

cottage industry 90-1
unique selling points 91
British Library, legal deposit 165-7
British Library Document Supply Centre 95-8
broadcast technologies *see* audiotex; videotex
browsing, printed journals 44-5, 53-4
budgetary constraints
Follett Review 2, 41, 169
libraries 2, 36-43, 169, 171-4
bulletin boards 138-9
user awareness 44, 47

Canada, research funding 1990-1992 23*fig*
CAS-IAS services 94, 102
CD-I
development costs 130
growth rate 161*fig*
market size 129-31
titles 130*fig*
United States 127
usage
leisure 129
research 131
see also CD-ROMS
CD-ROM players
market size 114-18
by country 115-17*fig*
United Kingdom 117, 118*fig*
schools 117

CD-ROM players (cont'd)
  usage 58-9
CD-ROMS
  abstract publishing 44
  full text databases 120, 124
  growth rate 118-20
    1987-1992 119*fig*
    1990-1995 119*fig*
    forecasts 160, 161*fig*
  leisure usage 124
  market size 114-18
  operating systems 113-14
  prices 122-5
  publishing 2, 113-14
    using SGML 76
  subjects 120-1, 122*tab*
  technology 113-14
  titles 118*fig*, 130*fig*
    by type 120*fig*, 121*fig*
    by use 121*fig*
  university libraries 39
  usage 116
    chemists 53
    leisure 124, 146
    versus Internet 114
  CD-I
Centre Européene de Recherche
  Nucléaire 29
change from paper to electronic
  media 1, 58
chemical articles, sources of information 54*fig*
Chemical Journals Online 52
Chemical Researchers User Study
  (CORE) 51-3
chemists, online searching 53, 55
commercial viability
  electronic infrastructure 58-9
  journal publishing 3
  neutral database publishing sys-
    tem 76
  new media ix, 169-70
  printed books 88-9, 91, 169-70
  printed journals 81-2, 84, 169-70

communications organizations
  publishing activities 85-6
  publishing partnerships 64-6
competition
  different media xii
  electronic publishing 171-4
  international research 24
  new media versus traditional
    media xii
computer aided production, current awareness services 76
conservatism, researchers 45-7,
  54-5, 60, 152
constraints
  budgetary 2, 36-43, 169
  publishing 7-8
    demography 8-12
    education 14-19
    employment trends 12-14
copyright
  library privilege 95, 97
  ownership 66
  printed versus electronic pub-
    lishing 85, 166-7
Copyright Clearance Center 81
Copyright Licensing Agency 81
cost
  CD-I 130
  digital storage 56
  inter-library loans 94
current awareness services 45
  computer aided production 76
  document delivery services 92-3
  prices 94

data collection methods 4-5
database searching *see* online
  searching
databases
  by type 110*fig*
  growth rate 107*fig*
  market developments 111-13
  publishers 111, 113*fig*

see also bibliographic databases; multimedia databases
decentralization
  journal publishing 64*tab*
  scholarly publishing 63-6
defence research 21
  United States 26
demography
  market size 152-3
  publishing constraints 8-12
developing countries
  population trends 9-11
  print publishing 154
  research funding 22
  subscriptions to printed journals
    81
development costs
  CD-I 130
  SGML 75-6
digital storage
  cost 56
  technology 57*tab*
DIY publishing, printed journals
  85
document delivery
  CAS-IAS services 94, 102
  electronic means 44
    stages of development 99*fig*
  library services 46
  photocopies 92
  prices 94, 102
  printed publications
    growth rate 95
    market size 92, 93*tab*, 102
    market value 93-5
    photocopies 92
    relation to electronic jour-
      nals 99
    relation to subscriptions 94
  royalties 93-4
  services 95*tab*
  stages of development 98-9,
    100-1*tab*
  see also inter-library loans;

printed journals
  Document Type Definition 76
  do-it-yourself publishing, printed
    journals 85
  dual publication, electronic and
    printed 143-4, 166

East Germany *see* Germany
economic competitiveness 24, 26
  economies of scale 64
  editorial content, electronic pub-
    lishing of printed works 166
education
  public expenditure 15*tab*
  publishing constraints 14-19
  scientists 27
electronic books 146-9
  hardware 148*fig*
  market size 146
  prices 147
  search and retrieval interfaces
    147
  Sony Data Discman 146-7
  titles 147, 148*fig*
  1993 list 186*tab*
electronic bulletin boards 138-9
  user awareness 44, 47
electronic document delivery 44
  bulletin boards 138-9
  growth rate 155-6
  preprints 138
  user expectations 52
  volume of traffic 156*fig*
electronic information services
  Europe 112*fig*
  informality 48
  international 73*fig*
  Internet 139-40
  usage by researchers 47*fig*
electronic infrastructure
  availability 49
  commercial viability 58-9

electronic journals 140-4
  acceptability by researchers 48
  dual publication 143-4, 166
  forecast growth 141
  market size 141, 142*fig*
  prestige 151
  relation to document delivery 99
  subjects 142-4
electronic publishing 103-4
  competition 171-4
  dual publication 143-4, 166
  effect of SGML 75-7
  Europe 78*fig*
  forecasts 162-3, 171-4
  legal deposit 166-7
  market forces 171-4
  ownership of rights 66
  see also bibliographic databases
electronic warehouse 76
Elsevier journal subscriptions 82*fig*
e-mail usage 45-7, 135
emerging subjects 31
employment trends 12-14
  women 12
Encapsulated PostScript 75
engineers
  bachelors degrees 16*fig*
  proportion of population 9*fig*
EUREKA programme 27-9
Europe
  audiotex 133
  bibliographic databases 105*fig*
  electronic information services
    112*fig*
  electronic publishing 78*fig*
  employment trends 12-13
  information industry 72*fig*
  intergovernmental research 29
  megascience 27
  multimedia publishing 127-8
  print publishing 74*fig*, 77*fig*
  research and development
    expenditure 28*tab*
    funding 26-9

  personnel 181*tab*
  student numbers 17*fig*
  see also individual countries,
    e.g. Germany; United Kingdom
European Union, research and de-
    velopment funding 27
expenditure
  printed books, United Kingdom
    86-8
  research and development, pro-
    portion of GNP 11*fig*
  export sales, printed books 88*fig*

fax-based publishing 144-5
Faxon Institute user studies 50-1
Follett Review
  availability of databases 112
  budgetary constraints 2, 41, 169
  publication rights 66
forecasting
  inconsistency 2
  methodology 4
  new media 1
forecasts
  electronic publishing 162-3,
    171-4
  growth rate
    BLDSC 97*tab*, 98*fig*
    electronic journals 141
    subscriptions 95
  online searching, United King-
    dom 157, 158*fig*
  print publishing 77-8, 154-5,
    162-3
  scholarly media 151-2
Foresight Programme 29
fragmentation
  journal publishing 64*tab*
  scholarly publishing 63-6
France
  public expenditure on education
    15*tab*

research and development funding 27
videotex 132, 158
free at the point of usage 50
freedom of information 66
full text databases on CD-ROMS 120, 124
funding *see* budgetary constraints; research and development

Game Theory 2
Germany
  population trends 12
  public expenditure on education 15*tab*
  research and development funding 27
  videotex 132
grey literature 85
gross domestic product, relation to research papers 10*fig*
gross national product 9-11
growth of knowledge *see* information explosion
growth rate
  bibliographic databases 106-8, 157*fig*
  BLDSC 97*tab*, 98*fig*
  CD-I 161*fig*
  CD-ROMS 118-20, 160, 161*fig*
  databases 107*fig*
  electronic document delivery 155-6
  electronic journals 141
  Internet 59, 134-5
  multimedia publishing 128*fig*
  networks 135*fig*
  online searching 157*fig*
  print publishing 154-5
    books 154*fig*
    journals 155*fig*
  research and development 31-5

subscriptions 95
videotex 159*fig*

handheld electronic books 146-7
hardware
  electronic books 148*fig*
  information technology 56, 57*tab*
higher education institutions
  library provision 18
  1986-1992 40*fig*
  student numbers 18

imbalance
  supply and demand viii, 41-3, 171-4
  new media 3
individual article supply 92-4, 102
individuals, payment for services 44, 50, 169, 172
industrial research 22
  Japan 31*fig*
information competency 51
information distribution systems 1
information explosion 7, 21, 56
  publishing 68-71
information industry 1
  data requirements 169-70
  Europe 72*fig*
  in-house organization 75
  Japan 72*fig*
  market forces 59
  market size 71-4
  trends viii, 151-2, 162-3
information needs of researchers, by subject 50-1
information overload, effect on individuals 14, 43
information technology
  current problems 55

information technology (cont'd)
hardware 56, 57*tab*
software 56
user-unfriendliness 55
see also technological change
in-house organization, information
industry 75
in-house publishing, international
corporations 91
interdisciplinary research 21-2
intergovernmental research in
Europe 29
inter-library loans 92
prices 94
see also document delivery
inter-media partnerships 64-6
international competition 24
international corporations, in-
house publishing 91
international electronic information industry 73*fig*
international publishing 1, 4
Internet x
commercial applications 139-40
electronic information services
139-40
financing 134
growth rate 59, 134-5
1992-1993 137*fig*
informality 48
navigators 139
publishing 2
search and retrieval systems 56
service types 136*fig*
usage
by service types 137*fig*
network documents 140*fig*
versus CD-ROMS 114
Internet Protocol *see* Transmission
Control Protocol/Internet
Protocol
Italy, research and development
funding 27

Japan
audiotex 133
industrial research 31*fig*
information industry 72*fig*
print publishing 74*fig*
private sector research 31*fig*
research funding 29-30
journal publishing
commercial viability 3
fragmentation 64*tab*
new titles 68, 68-9*fig*, 71*fig*
United States 36
see also research articles

knowledge warehouse 77

learned societies, printed journals
83
legal deposit, British Library 165-7
leisure usage
CD-I 129
CD-ROMS 124
libraries
budgetary constraints 2, 36-43,
169, 171-4
document delivery 46
expenditure on printed books
87*fig*
higher education institutions 18
1986-1992 40*fig*
library budgets
new media 37, 40*fig*
printed books 91
printed journals 84
United Kingdom 36-41, 39*tab*
United States 36, 42*fig*
library privilege, copyright 95, 97
life sciences versus physical sciences 24, 25*fig*
literature searching, printed journals 45

local area networks 134
Loughborough University, user
    studies 46-9

market forces
    databases 111-13
    electronic publishing 171-4
    information industry 59
    printed books 89*fig*, 91
    profitability xi
    supply and demand viii
market size
    audiotex 133, 159, 160*fig*
    bibliographic databases 104-6
    CD-I 129-31
    CD-ROM players 114-18, 118*fig*
    CD-ROMS 114-18
    demographic forecasts 152-3
    document delivery 92, 93-5,
        93*tab*
    electronic books 146
        hardware 148*fig*
    electronic journals 141, 142*fig*
    fax-based publishing 144
    information industry 71-4
    multimedia publishing 125,
        126*fig*
        Europe 127-8
        United States 127*fig*
    new media 171-4
    print publishing 74*fig*
    printed books 90
    printed journals 82-5
    videotex 132
megascience 21, 173
    Europe 27
    United States 23-4
Mexico, research funding, 1990-
    1992 23*fig*
migration from paper to electronic
    media 1, 58
military research *see* defence

research
Minitel 132, 158
Mosaic search and retrieval sys-
    tem 56
motivation of researchers 43, 46,
    70-1
multidisciplinary science 173
multimedia databases 109-10
multimedia publishing xi
    definition 125
    growth rate 128*fig*
    market size 125, 126*fig*
        Europe 127-8
        United States 127*fig*
    technology 125
    titles 128-9
    see also CD-ROMS; network
        publishing

National Science Foundation 134
natural sciences, bachelors degrees
    16*fig*
navigators (Internet) 139
network publishing xi, 134-40
    research articles 136
    see also Internet; World Wide
        Web
networks
    growth rate 135*fig*
    usage
        by biologists 48*fig*
        by researchers 46-7
        time element 141*fig*
neutral database publishing system
    76
new media ix
    commercial viability ix, 169-70
    competition xii
    forecasting 1
    library budgets 37, 40*fig*
    market size 171-4
    'out in the cold' researchers 43

new media (cont'd)
  publications during 1990s x*fig*
  supply and demand 3
  see also CD-ROMS; Internet;
    multimedia publishing; net-
    work publishing
new subjects 31, 68-70
new titles 68, 68-9*fig*, 71*fig*
  ALPSP survey 79*fig*
  electronic publishing of printed
    works 166
  printed books 88*fig*
new universities, library budgets
  39*tab*
non-uniform information technology 55

old universities, library budgets
  39*tab*
online searching
  by chemists 53, 55
  cost 44
  forecasts 157, 158*fig*
  growth rate 157*fig*
  United States 109*fig*
  university libraries 39-41, 113
  see also bibliographic databases
operating systems, CD-ROMS
  113-14
optical publications *see* CD-ROMS
'out in the cold' researchers 43, 51
ownership of publication rights 66

parallel publishing, electronic journals 143
partnerships in publishing 64-6
payment by individuals 44, 50,
  169, 172
peace dividend 22
peer review system 45-6

personal computers 58-9
photocopies 92
physical sciences versus life sciences 24, 25*fig*
population trends
  1980-2010 8*fig*
  developing countries 9-11
  Germany 12
  students 14-17
  United Kingdom 12
  United States 12
  young people 12-13
postgraduate students, science and
  engineering 1980-1990
  184-5*tab*
preprints 138
prestige
  electronic journals 151
  printed journals 45, 151
  researchers 45, 49, 60, 143, 173
  versus speed 49
prices
  CAS-IAS services 94, 102
  CD-ROMS 122-5
  document delivery 94, 102
  electronic books 147
  inter-library loans 94
  printed books 91
  printed journals 79, 85
print publishing 74-5
  competition xii
  dual with electronic publication
    143-4, 166
  Europe 74*fig*, 77*fig*
  forecasts 77-8, 154-5, 162-3
  growth rate 154-5
  Japan 74*fig*
  market size 74*fig*
  publications during 1990s x*fig*
  see also document delivery
printed books
  commercial viability 88-9, 91,
    169-70
  expenditure 86-8

export sales 88*fig*
growth rate 154*fig*
library budgets 91
market developments 89*fig*, 91
market size 90
new titles 88*fig*
prices 91
profitability 89*fig*
sales trends 87-9
titles published 90*fig*
United Kingdom 86-8
printed journals 44-5
abstracts 54
browsing 44-5, 53-4
commercial viability 81-2, 84,
169-70
decline 99, 102-3
DIY publishing 85
growth rate 155*fig*
leading publishers 83
literature searching 45
market size 82-5
peer review system 45-6
prestige 45, 151
prices 79, 85
profitability 81-2
royalties 81
subscriptions 78-81
university presses 83
see also document delivery
private sector research, Japan 31*fig*
profitability xi
printed books 89*fig*
printed journals 81-2
public expenditure, education
15*tab*
public libraries
book expenditure 38*fig*
budgets 37
publication rights 66
publish or perish 43, 70, 173
publishers
databases 111, 113*fig*
printed books

profitability 89*fig*
unique selling points 91
printed journals 83
Publishers Licensing Society 81
publishing
CD-ROMS 2, 113-14
change from paper to electronic
media 1, 58
constraints 7-8
demography 8-12
education 14-19
employment trends 12-14
cottage industry 63, 90-1
information explosion 68-71
inter-media partnerships 64-6
Internet 2
on demand 58
partnerships 64-6
United States, by medium 72*fig*
see also international publishing; journal publishing;
multimedia publishing; network publishing; scholarly
publishing

reading methods, chemical researchers 52
repackaging information xi
research and development
expenditure
Europe 28*tab*
proportion of GDP 25*fig*
proportion of GNP 11*fig*
funding 20-2, 60
by country 1961-1989
182-3*tab*
Europe 26-9
European Union 27
Japan 29-30
Mexico 23*fig*
North America 22-6
United Kingdom 29, 167

research and development (cont'd)
  growth by subjects 31-5
  numbers of personnel, Europe
    181*tab*
  perceived value 21
  small and medium firms 26-7
  value systems 21, 24
  see also particular types, e.g. de-
    fence research
research articles
  changing concept 103-4
  fax transmission 145
  network publishing 136
  sources of information 54*fig*
  subjects 32-3*tab*
    1973-1987 34*fig*
    by country 35*fig*, 67*fig*
  see also journal publishing
Research Councils 29
research information 1
research journals *see* printed jour-
    nals
research papers, relation to GDP
    10*fig*
research usage, CD-I 131
research versus study 19
researchers
  conservatism 45-7, 54-5, 60, 152
  information needs, by subject
    50-1
  integrity 26
  motivation 43, 46, 70-1
  need to publish 43, 46, 70-1, 173
  'out in the cold' 43, 51
  prestige 45, 49, 60, 143, 173
  self-perception 51
  usage
    electronic information serv-
      ices 47*fig*
    e-mail 45-7
    networks 46-7
  willingness to pay for services
    44, 50, 169, 172

resistance to change *see* conserva-
    tism
retrieval interfaces 56
Royal Society of Chemistry Study
    on Users 53-5
Royal Society Study on Scientific
    Information Systems 43-5
royalties
  printed journals 81
  relation to document delivery
    93-4

salami publishing 43
Schauder study 45-6
scholarly publishing
  forecasts 151-2
  fragmentation 63-6
  social factors 151-2
schools, CD-ROM players 117
scientific discoveries
  effect of market forces 172
  speed 21
scientists
  education, Europe 27
  manpower estimates 20*fig*
  numbers, Europe 181*tab*
  proportion of population 9*fig*
search and retrieval interfaces 56
  electronic books 147
separates *see* document delivery;
    research articles
serendipity *see* browsing
small and medium firms, research
    and development 26-7
small specialized publishers,
    printed journals 83
social factors, scholarly publishing
    151-2
software
  CD-ROMS 113-14
  information technology 56
Sony Data Discman 146-7

sources of information, chemical
articles 54*fig*
space race *see* megascience
speed
scientific discoveries 21
technological change 2
versus prestige 49
Standard Generalized Markup Language 75-7
STM journals *see* printed journals
Strathclyde University, user study
49-50
student numbers 14-17
Europe 17*fig*
higher education institutions 18
relation to demography 19*fig*
science and engineering graduates 1980-1990 184-5*tab*
United Kingdom 18-19, 153
first degree graduates 1989-
1995 180*tab*
university libraries 38
Study on Scientific Information
Systems, Royal Society
43-5
study versus research 19
subjects
audiotex 133
CD-ROMS 120-2
electronic books 147
electronic journals 142-4
research and development 31-5
research articles 32-3*tab*
1973-1987 34*fig*
by country 35*fig*
videotex 132-3
subscriptions
growth rate 95
printed journals 78-81
relation to document delivery 94
superhighways *see* Internet; World
Wide Web
supply and demand
balancing 2

imbalance viii, 41-3, 171-4
new media 3
market forces viii

Tagged Image File Format 75
technical manpower
estimates 20*fig*
Europe 181*tab*
technological change
speed 2
trends 57*tab*
see also information technology
technology
CD-ROMS 113-14
digital storage 57*tab*
fax transmission 145
multimedia publishing 125
see also information technology
telecommunications industry 3
publishing partnerships 64-6
see also electronic journals; network publishing
telecommunications organizations,
publishing activities 85-6
traditional media
competition xii
publications during 1990s x*fig*
see also print publishing
Transmission Control Protocol/Internet Protocol 135
twigging 31, 68-70

unique selling points of books 91
United Kingdom
bibliographic databases 112
CD-ROM players 117, 118*fig*
employment trends 13-14
expenditure on printed books
86-8
legal deposit 165-7

United Kingdom (cont'd)
  leisure expenditure 86*fig*
  library budgets 36-41, 39*tab*
  online searching 157, 158*fig*
  population trends 12
  printed books 86-8
  public expenditure on education
    15*tab*
  research funding 29, 167
  student numbers 18-19, 153
    first degree graduates 1989-
    1995 180*tab*
  videotex 159*fig*
United States
  Association of Research Librar-
    ies 41-2
  bibliographic databases 105*fig*
  CD-I 127
  defence research 26
  information industry 72*fig*
  journal publishing 36
  library budgets 36, 42*fig*
  megascience 23-4
  multimedia publishing 127*fig*
  online searching 109*fig*
  population trends 12
  print publishing 74*fig*
  public expenditure on education
    15*tab*
  publishing, by medium 72*fig*
  research and development, pro-
    portion of GDP 25*fig*
  research funding, 1990-1992
    23*fig*
  videotex 132
university libraries
  access strategy 41
  budgetary constraints 2, 36-43,
    169, 171-4
  collection development 38, 41
  databases
    availability 112
    searching 39-41, 113
university presses 83

usage
  bibliographic databases 108-9
  CD-I 129
  CD-ROM players 58-9
  CD-ROMS, leisure 124, 146
  electronic information services
    47*fig*
  e-mail 135
  Internet
    by service types 137*fig*
    network documents 140*fig*
    networks, by biologists 48*fig*
    personal computers 58-9
user studies 43-55
user-unfriendliness, information
  technology 55

value systems 21, 24
variations in information technology 55
videotex
  France 132, 158
  Germany 132
  growth rate, United Kingdom
    159*fig*
  market size 132
  subjects 132-3

West Germany *see* Germany
willingness to pay for services 44,
  50, 169, 172
women, employment trends 12
working age population 13*fig*
World Wide Web x
  search and retrieval systems 56

young people, population trends
  12-13